**Community Care
Practice Handbooks**

General Editor: Martin Davies

Contracts in Social Work

**Community Care
Practice Handbooks**

General Editor: Martin Davies

Contracts in Social Work

John Corden and Michael Preston-Shoot

Gower

COMMUNITY CARE
THE INDEPENDENT VOICE OF SOCIAL WORK

Published by
Gower Publishing Company Limited
Gower House
Croft Road
Aldershot
Hants GU11 3HR
England

Gower Publishing Company   '
Old Post Road
Brookfield
Vermont 05036
USA

British Library Cataloguing in Publication Data

Corden, John
    Contracts in social work.—(Community
care practice handbooks).
    1. Contracts—England   2. Public welfare
—Law and legislation—England
    I. Title   II. Preston-Shoot, Michael
    III. Series
    344.206′2′024362   KD1554

    ISBN 0-566-05130-3

Printed and bound in Great Britain by
Biddles Ltd, Guildford and King's Lynn

Contents

Acknowledgements

In developing our ideas and writing this book we have benefited from the encouragement and help of many people. David Asher, Sue Rockliffe, Carole Sellers and Pam Wilkinson, our colleagues in Leeds Family Service Unit, have offered helpful comments on drafts of the book. We have a substantial debt also to everyone who has worked at or is currently employed in Leeds Family Service Unit. Kay Barella and Jon Somerton, Leeds Social Services Department, and Harry Marsh, National Office, Family Service Units, also responded helpfully and critically to our ideas. Rosemary Bland, University of Stirling, and Julia Taylor and Jane Davies, Hertfordshire Social Services Department, enabled us to develop our thinking about contracts in the field of residential and day care. Many of the ideas in this book have been developed in workshops which we have run for Leeds Social Services Department. We would like to thank Ann Peasland from the training section of the Department and all those who have participated. Finally, we owe a considerable debt to those families and groups with whom we have worked. Their agreement to work with us has helped to shape this book. Although many of the illustrations are derived from work we have been involved in, we should make it clear that they do not represent necessarily the views of our employers.

John Corden and Michael Preston-Shoot

Introduction

This book is the outcome of a process of evolution. As practitioners, using contracts explicitly with individuals, families and groups, we have become aware that agreements akin to the idea of contracts are used frequently in social work. However, these agreements often do not fulfil our criteria for contracts but rather are a set of instructions imposed on consumers with a penalty clause for non-fulfilment and without any statement of what the practitioners are offering. As members too of the theoretical sub-culture (Sheldon, 1978) we have sought to develop our understanding of the concept of contract, its theoretical foundations and its uses in practice (Corden, 1980; Smith and Corden, 1981). Finally, to connect theory with practice and to promote an understanding and use of contracts in practice, we have organised several workshops on the theme of the making and breaking of contracts (Preston-Shoot *et al.*, 1984). This book, then, represents our latest thinking and practice experience. It is based on our interest and belief in contracts as a practical working concept, one which provides an effective and ethical basis for social work.

There are several reasons why a consideration of the use of contracts in social work practice now is particularly apposite. First, at a time when social work's contribution is being heavily scrutinised and challenged, our experience suggests that contracts enhance the process of social work and enable more effective outcomes. They are a means of avoiding time and energy being expended on double agendas and offer an opportunity to discuss and resolve clashes in perspective by giving consumers a chance to negotiate the rules for the intervention and an element of choice or role in the decision-making process. They are a means of clarifying and specifying the goals of intervention and of attempting to ensure that the social work process is purposefully related to these objectives. They are not something that evolves naturally as workers and clients interact, but are crucial in determining the quality of the relationship between the participants. Moreover, if contracts are a useful bridging concept between practitioners and clients, addressing the problems of miscommunication and different priorities which are fairly universal, they have a similar value for interactions between agencies and professionals. For example, in the field of child abuse, agreements are a practical way of ensuring coordinated action.

Secondly, social work has begun to integrate the implications of clients' rights and their involvement in the social work process through open records, attendance at case conferences and participation in policy-making and in the formulation of important decisions affecting them (BASW, 1980; Barclay, 1982; FSU, 1982). We believe that clients should be involved in deciding what the goals of the work are, in identifying what they want to achieve and what the worker thinks needs to be done. This implies that social workers do not necessarily know best and that all parties have an obligation to ensure that agreements are realistic and relevant, and to undertake the tasks thought necessary for a successful outcome. This implies too that it is not always necessary to have identical goals and that the unequal balance of power between professionals and consumers must and can be modified. Our practice experience has confirmed that contracts can enable social workers to operationalise the value principle of client involvement. They are perceived as useful by clients and encourage consumer participation by offering a sense of engagement, by enabling them to state and work on their objectives and by assigning responsibility for parts of the work to them. However, we have found also that clients are often unfamiliar with or sceptical about the rationale behind agreements and that social workers need to be more specific about the content and type of agreements reached (Preston-Shoot, 1985).

Thirdly, social work is a complex undertaking. It can involve competing or conflicting views within a family or group or between them and social workers. It can involve anxiety in the face of chaotic or frightening situations, together with choices about where to intervene, how, when and with whom. Increasingly, social workers are asked to make difficult decisions, for instance, in the field of child protection. We have found that clear agreements, and the process of the exchange of views which precedes them, may enable practitioners to contain their anxiety and retain direction in their work. Additionally, they may enable participants to explore each other's concerns prior to deciding on a course of action.

However, although some texts give the concept of contract a central place (Pincus and Minahan, 1973; Davies, 1981) or provide a paradigm and some practice guidelines (Corden, 1980; Sheldon, 1980; Smith and Corden, 1981), no work offers detailed guidance about ways in which contracts can be used daily in social work practice nor clarity about the many influences which, over time, have suggested or encouraged the development of this concept. As a result this practical concept could remain just an acknowledged 'good thing', happening much of the time but usually implicitly, unrecognised and open to incorrect use or misunderstanding. Indeed, we would agree that the concept of contract has been inadequately formulated and incompletely incorporated into practice. Little effort has been made to clarify its theoretical foundations, formulate a conceptual framework, delineate its uses and test its validity (Maluccio and Marlow, 1974).

Our purpose here is to stimulate interest in examining, conceptualising and using contracts explicitly in practice. We hope to achieve this aim in three ways. First, by producing a text which draws on social work theory and research which have encouraged interest in the concept of contract. Secondly, by spelling out the ingredients of the concept in some detail but in relatively simple language, particularly paying attention to the concept of contract in law and to the links and differences between this and the much looser concept which has begun to emerge in social work. Thirdly, by exploring the connections between this concept and practice by providing examples of how contracts may be used in practice and by discussing its range of applications. We shall deal with the issues involved in and the difficulties to be faced in agreeing contracts with individuals, couples, families and groups and between workers from different agencies. Other than some minor modifications to respect the requirement of confidentiality, all the examples given are taken from actual practice experience unless specifically stated in the text to be hypothetical. In summary, our purpose is to show how this theoretical concept fits practice across boundaries of method, setting and client group, and how the concept has developed out of theory.

The book falls into three sections. In the first two chapters we trace the origins and precursors of using contracts in social work practice, those influences which have led to the development of the concept of contract in social work. We believe this emphasis on theoretical and research foundations to be important even though social workers find it difficult to absorb theory or utilise research and often deny that such inputs have much relevance to their work (Carew, 1979). Practical working concepts develop out of sound theory. Theory and practice are not polar opposites and practitioners should have the opportunity to evaluate this concept by inspecting its foundations as well as the visible structure. Thus, in Chapter 1 we outline the contributions of the Functionalist School, task-centred social work, behaviour modification, the critique of institutional dependency and the development of the unitary approach. In Chapter 2 we discuss the interest in ascertaining the views and opinions of consumers and the important contribution to the development of contract theory of the emergence of the clash in perspective (Mayer and Timms, 1970). Given the evidence that many clients have felt unsure about the services they could expect to receive from social workers and the principle that clients have a right to be more actively engaged in decisions regarding the services they receive and the changes required of them, we believe that contracts are a means of mediating the clash in perspective without attempting to deny its existence and of giving consumers some role in making choices.

In Chapters 3, 4 and 5 our purpose again is to show that social workers can only understand and use theory if their knowledge base is documented and codified (Curnock and Hardiker, 1979). Therefore, we attempt to develop a fuller understanding of the nature of contracts. To achieve this we describe first the legal paradigm, identifying the essential ingredients which make up a contract and the rules which have evolved to ensure that parties are not exploited, have some redress and are not tied to inappropriate terms when circumstances change. In Chapter 3 also we attempt to identify the links and some of the differences between contracts in law and the looser concept of contracts in social work. In Chapter 4 we present a typology for and examples of using contracts in social work practice. We distinguish between contracts where the various parties share the same goals and those where worker and client have different aims in view. We contrast preliminary agreements to explore whether worker and client have a basis for any work together and major or substantive agreements based on a definition of goals. We distinguish between primary contracts which are formed between the key worker and the primary beneficiary and secondary contracts between the main parties and other persons or agencies whose cooperation is needed for the achievement of the goals identified in the primary contract. Finally, we make a distinction between the framework within which the work will take place and the substance, the part of the contract which sets out the main tasks to be accomplished by each party. In Chapter 5, to counterbalance the examples already given of contracts with individuals and families and to demonstrate this concept's applicability across different settings and methods, we look at the special features of using contracts in residential work and in working with groups.

The remaining chapters are concerned with practice issues. Chapter 6 offers a step-by-step model for the process of negotiating, implementing and, if necessary, revising a contract. Eight steps are described, the essential ingredients of each specified and connected with the legal concept presented in Chapter 3. The point will be made that these steps involve skills and processes already familiar to social workers. Chapter 7 gives detailed consideration to practice issues which arise when using contracts and to the conditions necessary for their effective use. In particular we examine criticisms and doubts which practitioners may have of this working concept and problems concerning the use of contracts with individuals, with family and marital systems, with other helping agencies and with groups of clients.

We hope that the reader will conclude that using contracts in their practice is feasible and important, that they have a workable structure for their practice and that they have an active knowledge base of how this concept has emerged within social work and how it can contribute to theory and practice.

1 Theoretical Foundations

Introduction
In this chapter the main theoretical influences on our working concept of contract are outlined. Some readers may regard this as unnecessary: why worry about the intellectual origins of an idea provided it is useful in practice? We do not hold this view but share the concern which has been expressed about the gap which has developed between the theoretical and practice 'sub-cultures' of social work (Sheldon, 1978; Carew, 1979).

Sheldon advocates the development of a cumulative knowledge base in social work, a store of 'working concepts' which can be changed or discarded as understanding develops. In our view, practical working concepts develop out of sound theory. Social workers rely on theory more heavily than they sometimes acknowledge but their knowledge base is rarely made explicit and, in respect of contracts, theory is in its infancy in social work (Curnock and Hardiker, 1979). We have attempted to identify the theoretical influences on which our working concept of 'contract' is based and the knowledge base which has led to the development of the concept in social work. Social workers have a right and a responsibility to examine the foundations as well as the visible structure of ideas they intend to apply to their practice.

Agency Function and the Functionalist School
In between the two World Wars, the image developed, particularly in America, of social work as a form of psychotherapy. It seems unlikely that many social workers were able to sustain this image in their practice. However, it had a profound influence, far beyond its relevance, on the training of social workers and on the direction of theory development.

The Functionalist School developed in reaction to this view. In a seminal article, Taft (1937) spelled out the crucial difference between psychotherapy and social work: therapists being required to take an individual responsibility for what they do; caseworkers' responsibility, on the other hand, first of all being to the agency and its function.

Howe reminds us that people do not normally become clients of social workers merely because they are suffering personal discomfort or distress but because their behaviour is giving cause for wider social concern or disapproval. Whilst acknowledging that many social work agencies are managed in ways which seem to inhibit the creative

1

application of social work principles, he casts serious doubt on the idea that social workers could somehow operate independently of their employing agencies which represent the wider community and provide a mandate for social work intervention (Howe, 1979). It follows that, when social workers are employed by agencies whose tasks and function are determined by the community, individual social workers will often have to engage in negotiations with their clients if they are to be able to work together towards a common goal.

The Functionalist School made a number of other contributions to social work theory. Rejecting the Freudian perspective which they criticised as offering a mechanistic and deterministic view of human beings, they relied instead on the ideas of Otto Rank. Once a pupil of Freud, Rank had broken away to establish his own school of psychotherapy. He believed in the purposeful nature of humanity. He saw people as capable of using human relationships and other experiences in their life to realise that purpose and to grow to maturity. The process of growth was not portrayed as necessarily being smooth or untroubled but the storm and stress of people's efforts to change were seen as opportunities for work rather than as symptoms of disturbance to be contained or cured.

According to this view, social workers were expected to leave individuals with the freedom to reach decisions and to return to their clients the responsibility for testing out their unique needs against the relatively stable function of a particular agency (Taft, 1937). Social workers were not seen primarily as emollients. They had a duty to facilitate the full experiencing of conflict which presently exists (Smalley, 1970).

The most relevant of the major principles of the Functionalist School to our working concept are summarised here:

1. Diagnosis is useful only in so far as it applies to the delivery of some particular form of service and when it is developed with the participation of clients and shared with them as appropriate.
2. The agency's function should not be camouflaged: it gives focus, content and direction to the social work process and ensures a proper accountability to society. It should make work more productive by generating the conflict out of which personal growth might come.
3. Social workers should be prepared to make deliberate use of 'structure' to further the effectiveness of the social work process. Informal chats are insufficient: a more formal examination of the issues is needed to ensure that clients are involved in identifying the options and taking the decisions.
4. All social work requires the use of relationship to engage the other in making and acting on choices and decisions. Unless clients are able to place some trust in their social worker as a person who

will respect their views even if they disagree with them, the work will achieve nothing (Smalley, 1970).

The strong links between the Functionalist School and the emerging concept of contract are highlighted in the view that the social worker's task in the 'beginning phase' and the goal in any beginning is to find a common base for worker and client to work together towards a common purpose, with the rules of the game known, and its elements broken down into what can be encompassed for immediate engagement (Smalley, 1970).

Task-centred Social Work

This model of practice was developed in the 1960s. Originally it was based on the findings of an experiment which compared the impact of planned short-term help with that of traditional open-ended casework (Reid and Shyne, 1969). Out of this work a more specific model was formulated, central to which was the requirement that the problem on which workers decided to concentrate was one which clients explicitly acknowledged and were prepared to work on (Reid and Epstein, 1972). In their model this is regarded as more important than the view of the agency or of the worker as to the nature of the problem. The model also prescribes that whatever problem is selected for attention, it should be one which lies within the combined resources of worker and client together to resolve. Like Taft and Smalley, Reid and Epstein base their model on a belief that people are purposeful beings who can exercise some control over their immediate environment. Successful problem-resolution should bring with it additional benefits in that the experience should leave clients feeling more confident to tackle subsequent problems unaided.

As a reaction against the then prevailing assumption that clients could be helped only through the medium of a therapeutic relationship which had to be sustained over a long period, Reid and Epstein's work offered a healthy counterbalance. According to their model, worker and client would agree on a problem to be addressed in the first or second interview. This problem then would be broken down into a series of tasks to be completed by the worker and client, mostly by the client. Each success was to be acclaimed and each failure analysed. Overall success was determined by the extent to which the original problem had been alleviated. The whole process was recommended to last not more than four months from beginning to end with about twelve contacts between social worker and client.

However, the model in its original form also suffered from two major limitations both of which, in our view, are symptomatic of the authors' relative neglect of agency function. The first limitation involves their exclusion of certain categories of problem and, consequently, of people as unsuitable for this model on the grounds that they would not respond to short-term methods. This is not unreasonable in itself but when the model is not designed to help people suffering from neurosis, character disorders, alcoholism, drug addition and the like (Reid and Epstein, 1972), we feel that they have imposed a major limitation on the value of this model for social workers in British statutory agencies. Although only a minority of any social worker's caseload may attract one or more of these labels, it is usually the minority who absorb a disproportionate amount of the social worker's time and energy. A model which has nothing to offer social workers in these areas is liable to be dismissed as irrelevant.

The second limitation concerns the primary requirement that the work should focus only on problems which the client acknowledges and is willing to work on in the first two interviews. This requirement, apart from the time constraint, is also a key principle of the non-treatment paradigm advocated recently for probation officers (Bottoms and McWilliams, 1979). In his later work Reid seems to acknowledge the limitations this requirement imposes by placing less emphasis on the time constraint and by recognising the need for a 'pre-client stage' when the worker and the person seeking help explore the issues constituting the problem to ascertain whether they can reach agreement (Reid, 1978). However, the general emphasis in this model on the client's right to determine what problem the work should address does not fit easily with the reality that, in Britain at least, most referrals to social work agencies are made by people other than the designated client as a result of the concern they experience about another person's behaviour, concern which often is not shared by the client.

So, while the task-centred model has been tested in Britain, with some success in contexts where it has been possible to mount a piece of systematic evaluative research (Goldberg and Robinson, 1977; Butler *et al.*, 1978; Gibbons *et al.*, 1979), it has not spread widely into the day-to-day work of ordinary practitioners. Its indirect influence, both on the teaching of social work and on the delivery of social services, has been considerable nevertheless. The model's approval of short-term intervention, its emphasis on limiting intervention to realistic and attainable goals, and its insistence on limiting intervention to problems which the client acknowledges, can all be seen to have influenced social work practice, even of those who would claim never to have heard of the model. The importance of frequent and regular contact, of systematically focusing on the agreed problem, and of assigning certain tasks to client and worker alike has been less widely recognised, while the emphasis on the need for careful evaluation of outcomes has been ignored almost totally.

Behaviour Modification
Over the last twenty years this means of achieving change has made a considerable impact on social work, particularly in the areas of children's behaviour problems, adult psychiatric disorder, and skill-

training for the mentally handicapped. Major works have been written which offer precise and detailed instructions for social workers wishing to use this method (Fischer and Gochros, 1975; Gambrill, 1977) and simpler accounts have been provided for the British market (Herbert, 1981; Sheldon, 1982).

Although over the same period social workers have been subjected to numerous demoralising studies claiming to show that they achieve no positive change, ironically it is the apparent power of behaviour modification to bring about change which tends to generate suspicion amongst British social workers who criticise its mechanistic assumptions. Partly as a reaction to such criticism, though from different sources, and partly because the advocates of learning theory have begun themselves to develop a more sophisticated set of assumptions about human beings' relationship with their environment, clinical psychologists have begun to rely on 'contracts' to sanction their intervention.

Fischer and Gochros (1975) offer three reasons for recommending that practitioners intending to use behaviour modification techniques begin by drawing up an 'intervention contract'. First, they argue that if a client knows about a treatment procedure and expresses willingness to participate in it, the treatment is more likely to succeed. Secondly, they claim that knowing precisely what it is that one has to learn has been shown to lead to more successful learning. Finally, they acknowledge that practitioners are on firmer ground, from an ethical point of view, when they are open and explicit about the treatment they intend to administer.

The use of rewards or punishments deliberately to encourage certain behaviours and discourage others is clearly open to abuse in some contexts. In residential social work, for example, there are establishments where the workers may have such extensive influence over the general quality of life that residents may feel unable to refuse to participate in a behaviour modification programme. In such situations contracts can be the instrument by which the rights of all parties are made explicit and, to some extent, protected. However, in the standard texts on this method, the contract is seen as secondary and subsidiary to the method or technique being offered. It is, we feel, taken for granted that the help to be made available will be a form of behaviour modification. The contract is seen first as a means of enhancing the effectiveness of the method and, almost as an afterthought, as a means of securing the client's consent.

For social workers, we consider that this approach has got things back to front. In our view, the process of negotiating the contract is what should determine the methods by which agreed problems are to be tackled. In any event, behaviour modification alone does not seem to work for everybody. Two practitioners who rely heavily on this approach have identified four factors where in their experience failure has occurred most frequently and which might predict failure:

1. The child has a long history of behaviour problems and especially when these are delinquent in type.
2. The family presents with multiple and chronic problems including social isolation and low motivation.
3. The parents have personality problems.
4. The therapy requires the united cooperation of several environmental systems, such as school, home and community (McAuley and McAuley, 1980).

This list is perhaps even more comprehensive in the categories it excludes from the hope of successful change than that of Reid and Epstein. No prizes are awarded for working out who ends up with responsibility for these 'untreatable' cases!

The Critique of Institutional Dependency

Just as social workers in community-based settings have been influenced by the ideas described above, so residential social workers have also seen major changes of emphasis and approach. Beginning with the critiques of large impersonal residential institutions for small children (Spitz, 1945; Goldfarb, 1945; Spitz, 1946; Bowlby, 1951), residential work has been influenced also by the severe criticisms levelled at certain kinds of institution for adults (Goffman, 1961; Barton, 1966). The critique of institutional care for small children concentrated on their inability to provide stable adult attachments for each individual child. The critique of 'total institutions' for adults alleged that the effect of the regimes in these supposedly therapeutic institutions was to exacerbate the difficulties in functioning which had led to the inmates' admission in the first place. The very low levels of social functioning displayed by many residents were claimed not to be a consequence of their illness but of an environment which created dependency and ran more smoothly when the inmates were submissive and apathetic.

One response to both critiques was to develop smaller family-type units. Family Group Homes for children, for example, were a major and, in many respects, successful development in residential child-care although even in these establishments attempts to maintain a family atmosphere were eroded as the principle of maintaining children's links with their natural families was given greater priority. Gradually, children's homes became used increasingly as refuges or staging-posts from which a return home or a placement with foster-parents could be planned (Berridge, 1985).

In homes and hostels for adults, however, the sense of family was harder to sustain in reality although the image may often have seemed more seductive. In an article on regimes in after-care hostels, Griffiths criticises weaknesses of the family model on the basis that the claim of family can never be a reality: the drawback in offering a deprived person a family experience is that he might accept it and become your child. Griffiths claims that a major factor in the high turnover of staff is the stress of tolerating the demands of men whose expectations have been falsely aroused. To become a parent is not a job but a way of life (Griffiths, 1970).

One study of homes for chronically sick adults identified two contrasting models of practice. The 'warehousing' model emphasised the need to prolong the lives of residents at the cost of imposing unreasonable restrictions on their freedoms. The 'horticultural' model, on the other hand, involved encouraging residents to lead a 'normal' life, efforts being made to cultivate the residents' potential for growth at the cost of denying the real restrictions which their illnesses imposed (Miller and Gwynne, 1975).

The institutions examined in this study are, in one sense, unique in that, unlike most other systems, they produce no identifiable output. Their task, as the authors bluntly describe it, is to help residents make the transition from social to physical death. This poses special problems for the staff since what is intolerable about this task is that it might imply that the individuals could have a choice about when to die. The solution these authors propose to cope with this intolerable situation is the development of an 'organisational' model for such homes, geared to a recognition that residents have differing and sometimes contradictory needs. Practice which was based on this model would make it possible for residents to decide for themselves how to respond to and cope with their chronic illness. Further, it would enable staff to acknowledge these individual preferences: for dependence in some areas, independence in others.

Although these institutions are unique in one respect, in others they share many of the stresses and dilemmas common to all forms of residential care. In the search for alternative approaches which has been stimulated by these critical evaluations, there has been increased recognition of the importance of identifying and responding to individual need, of involving residents in decision-making, and of being explicit about the conditions on which residents were accepted into homes and hostels. The concept of contract has been advocated by several contributors to this debate (Personal Social Services Council, 1975; Corden, 1976; Hall, 1980; Norman, 1980; Ward, 1980; Bland and Bland, 1985).

The Development of the Unitary Approach
In the early 1970s attempts were made to define a common core of skills and knowledge which could be used as the foundation for the training of all social workers. These formulations, which rapidly became known collectively as the 'unitary approach', originated in America (Goldstein, 1973; Pincus and Minahan, 1973; Middleman and Goldberg, 1974) but

were rapidly taken up, analysed and critically evaluated by British writers and practitioners.

There are many important differences between the various models of practice. In this brief discussion we shall concentrate mainly on the common elements, with particular reference to the work of Pincus and Minahan which, in our view, represents both the clearest account and the model which is most easily applied to a British context.

The crucial difference between these approaches and the models which preceded their arrival is their view of the relationship between clients and their problems. In varying degrees they challenge the assumption that the presence of a problem in a client's life necessarily indicates the existence of personal pathology in the client. Without needing to resort to Marxist ideology, these models explicitly acknowledge that many of the problems experienced by clients are results of failures in systems other than the client-system or of failures in the interaction between the client and the other system. While drawing attention to these different perspectives, they do not rule out the possibility that some problems may be located entirely within the system of which the client is a member.

Along with this broader perspective for the analysis and understanding of problems, the frameworks offered by the 'unitary approach' all rely on a view of human beings which closely resembles the Rankian view borrowed by the functionalists: people are seen as purposeful, goal-oriented individuals with the capacity to take decisions and make choices in respect of their own lives. However, they acknowledge that many clients' energy and inner resources have been undermined by the effects of structural disadvantage. The social work task, therefore, is seen as often involving a process of engaging with systems other than the client-system, though usually with the active participation of the client. This process of engagement with other systems is seen by Pincus and Minahan in particular as a process involving negotiation, bargaining and the establishment of contracts or working agreements.

The starting point for the 'unitary approach' is that it is a mistake to train social workers exclusively in one method or skill since problems rarely reach practitioners in a form which conveniently fits the area in which they happen to be skilled. Most problems, if they can be alleviated at all, are susceptible to more than one approach and much depends on what the client and the other parties find acceptable as a method of achieving change. Thus, the processes of exploration, assessment and contract negotiation are crucial. Decisions about how to intervene depend not only on the professional skills possessed by the worker but also on the preferences of the client and the priorities of the agency to which the worker is contracted.

This more complex view of the nexus of relationships with which the social worker has to work inevitably places greater emphasis on the negotiating process. All three major contributors recognise the importance of contracts although, to varying degrees, they portray them as understandings which develop naturally in the course of the work rather than as instruments by which social workers can actively enhance their clients' power to influence outcomes and accelerate the process of change. Goldstein (1973) seems to assume that contracts somehow emerge without any initiative on the worker's part, that as norms evolve out of the professional encounter and fall into some configuration, they can be understood and referred to as contracts. Middleman and Goldberg (1974), whose bias throughout is on bringing about improvements in clients' external environments, rule out the idea that it could be useful to introduce written agreements into social work, instead using the term 'contract' metaphorically to indicate that worker and client have verbally agreed upon what will be done and how. Even Pincus and Minahan (1973), who claim to regard the skill of negotiating contracts as central to their foundation course for social work students, and who devote a whole chapter to aspects of this skill, seem reluctant to emphasise the role of the social worker in actively negotiating contracts. They explain that they use the term to call attention to the existence of such working agreements between the parties to a change-effort whether or not the social worker and the other systems explicitly recognise them. However, elsewhere they give a higher priority to the concept. They restrict the use of the term 'client' to refer to people who have asked for help, are the intended beneficiaries of the change-effort and have an agreed contract with the practitioner. Unlike Reid and Epstein, Pincus and Minahan do not require that clients acknowledge the existence of a problem and express a willingness to work on it: the contract may define the problem as being outside the clients' area of influence or responsibility and one which the social worker offers to tackle with others. This difference of position is subtle but crucial. Although Pincus and Minahan refer to the contract between the practitioner and the client as the primary contract, they recognise the existence of and need for contracts between the social worker and other systems which may have contributed to the problem or hold the resources necessary to alleviate it.

It is curious that the few British accounts of attempts to implement the unitary approach make little reference to the task of negotiating contracts as a central part of their work (Coulshed, 1980; Currie and Parrott, 1981; Holder and Wardle, 1981). This may indicate that the work of writers such as Pincus and Minahan has had, as yet, only a superficial impact on British social work practice and that the gap between the theory and practice sub-cultures mentioned in this chapter's introduction has not yet been bridged in this respect.

Conclusion
This chapter has examined the main theoretical influences which have helped to formulate the concept of contract. The next chapter will

2 Clients: Their Opinions and Their Rights

Introduction

The concept of contract which emerges through the unitary approach implies that contracts arise naturally as a by-product of the client–worker relationship. However, we believe that the task of negotiating contracts is crucial in determining the quality of this relationship and that social workers have a responsibility and opportunity to ensure that agreements are as clear and open as situations allow. This process offers clients an opportunity to help set the rules which will govern subsequent transactions. It requires social workers to relinquish some power by offering clients an element of choice and an active role in decision-making. Recently, there has been growing pressure to alter the power balance which exists between clients and practitioners. This pressure has come from studies of clients' attitudes towards social workers and the help they provide and from the growing movement representing clients as consumers of social services. This has demanded greater attention to the rights of clients as citizens. In this chapter we shall review those main features of these two influences which seem relevant to the concept of contract.

Studies of consumer opinion began to be taken seriously when the psychoanalytic concepts on which social work theory had been built, and which encouraged practitioners to interpret clients' views as symptoms of psychological disturbance, began to be questioned (Shaw, 1976). The movement to articulate clients' rights was linked to the wider interest in the rights of consumers which developed from the late 1960s. Both developments were informed by and provided ammunition for the radical critique of social work which acquired considerable momentum in the 1970s (Jones, 1975; Statham, 1978; Corrigan and Leonard, 1978; Simpkin, 1979; Brake and Bailey, 1980; Walker and Beaumont, 1981).

Studies of Client Opinion

Studies of client opinion were once almost totally neglected as an area of systematic enquiry (Mayer and Timms, 1970). Now the position has been transformed to the point where it is difficult to conduct respectable research without incorporating the client's viewpoint (Fisher, 1983). However, quantity does not necessarily ensure quality. Research in this area must surmount some fundamental difficulties. The very idea of evaluating the quality of services provided by social workers is alien to many clients whose attitudes are based on the assumption that the services they receive are favours rather than entitlements. Many clients do not believe that they have any right to criticise or make judgements (Shaw, 1976). Clients often have very different perceptions of the boundaries of service, what is and is not the social worker's business, from their social workers. Often they see their status as clients as permanent, in contrast to practitioners who invest heavily in the belief that clienthood is a transitional state. Moreover, most consumer studies are designed by people whose perceptions and beliefs are much closer to those of social workers than clients. Consequently, the questions are based on a social work frame of reference. The subjects are handicapped by their limited knowledge of alternative responses which might have been made to their difficulty and they are, therefore, unlikely to feel able to make suggestions which fall outside the frame of reference built into the survey (Phillimore, 1982).

The design of consumer studies can also distort our awareness of clients' views. Interviewers often rely on the most accessible member of a client-system to answer their questions who, in family settings, is usually the female caretaker. Some studies fail to clarify who is the 'real' client, whose opinions are being sought, or to define clearly what constitutes client-satisfaction. This is a difficult task. A high level of satisfaction can coexist with a substantial element of criticism. When clients' expectations are very low they may report a high level of satisfaction with the service at the same time as expressing a high level of unresolved personal discomfort. Clients also reveal discrepancies between 'helpful people' and 'useful outcomes' so that they may report that their social worker was helpful but remain dissatisfied about the outcome. Alternatively, they may regard the outcome as satisfactory whilst expressing dissatisfaction about how they were treated personally (Shaw, 1984). In many studies the information is collected only after a significant time-lapse without any check on the reliability of the informants' recall. Often samples are small, sometimes biased and in many cases not even clearly described. Many authors fail to place their clients' accounts of their experiences with social workers in the context of their previous experiences of seeking help or of the general attitudes in their informal networks towards social workers and welfare agencies.

These criticisms of consumer studies (see Shaw, 1976; Rees and Wallace, 1982; Fisher, 1983; Shaw, 1984) are not all easily remedied. However, they illustrate the highly provisional nature of knowledge about clients' opinions. This is partly because, traditionally, social worker–client interaction has not encouraged clients to express their views. The introduction of contracts into social work is one means of changing that state of affairs. For that reason we shall review the main findings of consumer studies in so far as they might have some bearing on our concept.

An overriding theme of the studies has been that a 'clash in perspective' can often be identified between worker and client and is frequently associated with a high level of client dissatisfaction. It has not been found in all social worker–client interactions (Day, 1981; Sainsbury *et al.*, 1982). However, it is extremely pertinent to practitioners interested in the concept of contract. If social workers and their clients always saw the situation identically, there would be little call for a process of negotiation in which an attempt was made to define the rights and duties of each party. We shall examine four explanations for this clash in perspective.

Social Class

Mayer and Timms (1970) regarded social class as the most powerful single factor explaining the clash in perspective. They reported that when clients brought problems of interpersonal relationships they expected practitioners to adjudicate in the dispute, take the side of the 'injured' party and/or persuade the 'delinquent' family members to moderate their conduct. Dissatisfied clients were bewildered by the social worker's attempts to provide them with insight into their problem. Not only did the worker and client approach the problem from very different viewpoints, but clients were almost totally unaware that the worker's approach to problem-solving was fundamentally different from their own. The social workers were unaware that the clients entered the treatment situation with a different mode of problem-solving.

Other clients came to the agency with severe financial problems. Those who were dissatisfied with the treatment they received complained that workers seemed to disregard their financial plight and sought detailed information about their marital and family circumstances which seemed irrelevant to the clients. Thus, the social workers and the dissatisfied clients approached each other with quite different sets of assumptions about how those problems should be addressed. Neither party seemed to realise that their assumptions were not identical. Mayer and Timms attributed this to the different cultural traditions of middle-class social workers and working-class clients. Consequently, they were deeply pessimistic about the possibility of achieving any change.

Rees (1978) offered a different perspective. He found that some clients strongly believed that seeking help from social workers was shameful. However, clients were able to work through these feelings except where social workers, often under acute pressure to contain and control their workload, applied judgements which the clients perceived as confirming their sense of shame and worthlessness. This view, that working-class clients often come to an agency with a sense of stigma which will evaporate if they get a response which conveys respect and a belief in their value as people, is confirmed by our experience. Our view is that stereotyped attitudes to problems do vary according to social class but that these often form only the surface layer, the initial reaction

made in strange and unfamiliar situations. We encounter many workers
from middle-class backgrounds who subscribe to the 'unicausal–
moralistic–suppressive' attitude[1] to interpersonal problems which
Mayer and Timms ascribe to working-class clients. Equally, our
experience suggests that many working-class clients, once they have
established a degree of trust in their worker, will acknowledge that they
themselves may be contributing to the maintenance of an interpersonal
problem.

The issue is important because if these attitudes are part of a deeply-
rooted view of the world held by the working class, social workers have
to decide whether to accept and work within that worldview, or to try to
change it. We would share Mayer and Timms' pessimism about the
likely success, let alone the ethics, of major 're-education' programmes
which aimed to enable clients to see their problems from the perspective
of middle-class social workers. However, given Rees's argument that
the sense of shame and disgrace felt by the client is at the root of the
stereotyped attitudes, the 'clash in perspective' might be alleviated in
three ways. First, by establishing semi-formal processes in which the
possibility of working with clients as partners is explored. Secondly, by
specifically acknowledging the fears which clients might have about the
nature of social work involvement in their lives. Thirdly, by a process of
contract-making to safeguard clients' rights and to spell out their
responsibilities as partners in the problem-solving process.

Ignorance
Several studies have shown clearly that many potential and actual
clients lack clear knowledge or information about the services provided
by social work agencies. Thus:

1. The more familiar clients are with the functions of an agency, the
   more help they expect from it (McKay *et al.*, 1973). Many clients
   have had little information about services which social workers
   could offer and their ignorance affects their access to these and
   related services (Rees, 1978).
2. Few clients seek help of their own initiative. Many more, referred
   by a third party, are contacted in the first instance by a social
   worker. Many do not know prior to the practitioner's visit what
   help, if any, they could expect and what services are provided
   (McKay *et al.*, 1973; Burck, 1978). This level of ignorance extends
   to the people who refer them to social work agencies. For them it
   may serve a function, it being easier to stereotype social work as
   something to do with people who have not been successful, who in
   some way are deviant, than to find out (Rees, 1978).
3. Clients often think they are still receiving help when in the view of
   the agency their cases have been closed, and vice versa. Different
   views are often held about who was responsible for terminating

contact (McKay *et al.*, 1973; Burck, 1978).

4. Most clients are not given clear information by the referring workers about the kind of help other agencies would offer and intense feelings often surround the events which precipitate referral, frequently leading to a sense of apprehension and suspicion towards social workers (Sainsbury, 1975; Phillimore, 1981).

The implications of these findings for good practice are clear. Social workers must be ready to spend considerable time and effort, when they first meet a client, explaining and giving information about the services they can provide. The use of well-designed and easily read leaflets to provide basic information before contact is made might help to alleviate the problem. However, social workers also need to be aware that the initial reaction of clients when they make contact may often be influenced by the sense of confusion and uncertainty they feel.

Professional–Client Interactions
Encounters between high-status professionals and their clients are delicate pieces of interaction. Encounters between doctors and their patients include features which seem particularly difficult to manage— for instance, the distressing nature of some of the information which has to be communicated and the high levels of anxiety experienced by patients (Robinson, 1978). These difficulties cannot be attributed primarily to social class differences since middle-class patients, and particularly the parents of sick or handicapped children, have been amongst the most vociferous critics.

Studies of consumers' views of social workers have indicated that the peculiar nature of professional–client interaction, and the reactions of professionals to the emotional undertow of clients' initial reactions, make a specific contribution to the 'clash in perspective'. For example, in one study of families attending a child guidance clinic, the crucial differences between satisfied and dissatisfied clients at the 'contract-making' stage were that the satisfied clients, whilst doubtful of the social worker's assessment, were more open to consider explanations other than their own and felt valued and supported. The dissatisfied clients, whether or not they disagreed with the focus on their contribution to the problem, both asserted their view that the child should be the focus for treatment and saw the social work assessment as an attack on their competence as parents and even as persecutory. While this group may have brought more vulnerable self-esteem and greater mistrust, the social worker responded by confrontation, easily interpreted as attack, rather than by support and valuing (Lishman, 1978).

Another aspect of professional–client interaction is how far and at what point the professional's assessment should be shared with the client. In one study, a substantial measure of agreement on the purpose of the social work effort was found between social workers and clients in the early stages of their work. Agreement was greatest where social workers concentrated on areas of practical and immediate concern. In many cases, the workers had also set themselves the objective, initially not shared with the client, of bringing about improvements in family functioning. When these aims remained undisclosed for a long period, three difficulties were liable to arise. First, the social worker's style or approach began to feel irrelevant to the client. Secondly, some clients began to complain that the work seemed aimless. Thirdly, some clients reported a significant loss of morale following the improvements they had reported initially (Sainsbury *et al.*, 1982).

These findings are partly attributable to the perceived power or dominance of the professional over the client, particularly in the area of making judgements or assessments. They point social workers towards being more open about their assessments and paying more attention to clients' reactions to these assessments.

Formal Power and Authority
Having considered the effect of the power ascribed to professionals by clients on account of their special expertise and status, another feature of social work which contributes to the 'clash in perspective' and often has a greater impact on clients is the formal power invested in practitioners by statutes. Studies of children in a local authority assessment centre (Reinach and Roberts, 1979), and of foster-parents' views of social workers (Shaw and Lebens, 1977), both suggest that in many respects the participants are living in different worlds. The young people in care had only the most limited understanding of the purposes of their stay and seemed to learn only by accident, often from other residents, why and for how long they were there. Decisions or plans to move them to other establishments were rarely shared with the young people concerned in a positive manner and often would be implemented suddenly and without preparation. The study of foster-parents showed that they valued many aspects of their social worker's contribution, particularly qualities of warmth, encouragement and support. However, when it came to the exercise of professional judgement, particularly at times of pain and conflict, such as when the placement was in danger of breakdown, the foster-parents clearly did not have a high regard for this aspect of their social worker's skills. With issues of power and responsibility, for example regarding children returned 'home on trial' to their parents or concerning work with foster-parents when a placement is near the point of breakdown, social workers have to maintain a delicate balance between helping people work through their feelings and regain their confidence whilst also monitoring the progress of the children. Social workers are often criticised for failing to maintain this balance (Beckford Report, 1985). Thoburn's account of the experiences of parents whose children had been removed by the local

authority and then returned 'home on trial' indicated that the parents want social workers to be honest with them about what they are planning for their children and to do what they say they will do or explain why they could not. They want them to empathise: to listen and to try to understand how they feel. They want them to be caring, helpful and sometimes controlling towards their children (Thoburn, 1980).

Another situation in which social workers are vested with considerable discretionary power is in the preparation of social enquiry reports for offenders about to appear in juvenile court. In a high proportion of cases courts will implement the recommendations of social enquiry reports (Thorpe and Pease, 1976; Hine *et al.*, 1978). One study of clients' views here found numerous instances in which social workers made assumptions which were not shared by their clients. For example, in their approach to an imminent court appearance, the social workers appeared to regard the process as routine and one in which the outcome was highly predictable and essentially a formality. Not surprisingly, this was not how the families approached it but the social workers seemed to pay little attention to their anxieties (Parker *et al.*, 1981).

Some findings in this area have been more positive. Two studies found that clients of Family Service Units were well aware that, in spite of the informality with which FSU social workers maintained relationships, they exercised power also. Their ability to cut through the red tape of other agencies and to exercise influence on clients' behalf was seen as the most significant benefit of having a social worker (Phillimore, 1981). Clients saw social workers as using their power to bring about change within the family and felt that they had given permission to social workers to operate in this way (Sainsbury, 1975). This study also found that families expressed approval of social workers who anticipated problems and offered help in areas other than those designated as problematic at the time of referral, and who appeared to think about needs and help in the same way as they did. However, clients did not expect their workers to 'talk the same language' or to do everything asked of them. These clients would not, it seems, be comfortable holding total responsibility for designating the 'target problem' (Reid and Epstein, 1972) or with the 'non-treatment paradigm' in which probation officers are urged to refrain from offering help to clients except in those areas where it is explicitly requested (Bottoms and McWilliams, 1979).

Studies of Client Opinion: A Summary and Proposals for Change

Familiar themes emerge from these studies. Clients want their views to be taken into account. They want to be treated with respect as people capable of being reasonable and responsible, to be involved in the process of planning and decision-making. However, they accept that social workers must exercise some power. They welcome social workers who anticipate problems, make suggestions and initiate action to deal with them, provided they are open about their concerns and intentions and do not act without consultation.

We have discussed some of the factors contributing to the 'clash in perspective' which often develops between clients and practitioners. The recognition of this phenomenon is part of a growing awareness that miscommunication between people from differing backgrounds is endemic and not necessarily a symptom of deep-rooted psychological difficulties (Sheldon, 1980). Misunderstandings are normal hazards of everyday life, exacerbated by the different sets of assumptions held by clients and social workers.

Not only have social workers become more self-critical of claims that they have a unique and special expertise to offer but also they have become more aware of clients' abilities to assess their own needs, based on a belief that clients can make choices and take decisions in a sensible and responsible manner when they are given good information about the range of options open to them (Mullender and Ward, 1985).

Consumer studies also make other recommendations about ways in which practice could be altered to take account of their findings. Some studies underline the importance for clients of receiving a rapid and appropriate response to their practical and material problems, even where it is felt that these may indicate more deep-seated problems in family functioning. Practitioners should take seriously and treat with respect the problems presented to them (Mayer and Timms, 1970; Sainsbury, 1975). Services should be adapted to take account of the cultural expectations of client groups. Intervention should be crisis-oriented, clearly focused on the presenting problem. Help should be offered over a short time-scale with the option for clients to seek further help if needed. Practitioners should use examples which are familiar to clients and intervention should be based on the values, needs and desires of the client (Skynner, 1976; Burck, 1978; Mullender and Ward, 1985). Easier access to offices should be provided, together with much wider publicity and explanation of the kind of help social workers can offer and of why they proceed as they do. This includes preparing clients for the approach that they will encounter (Burck, 1978; Lishman, 1978). By increasing clients' awareness of the available services, their bargaining power will grow too (McKay *et al.*, 1973).

Some studies recommend a shared approach to goal-setting: working agreements which define shared aims (McKay *et al.*, 1973) and ensure that clients know both the social workers' short- and long-term goals and the links between them (Sainsbury, 1975). They should incorporate time-limits and the designation of individual and joint tasks (Sainsbury *et al.*, 1982). Reviews of agreed aims, where practitioners feed back their perceptions explicitly, might counter the blaming dynamic experienced by clients (Lishman, 1978).

Underlying almost all these proposals is the need for worker and client to establish trust. The social worker's style and manner are crucial in shaping the nature of the relationship and in helping clients feel confident that they are dealing with a person of integrity. A number of specific issues concern clients: anxiety about the extent of a social worker's statutory powers, confidentiality, record-keeping and fears about secret decision-making. Any model of practice, designed to take consumers' views into account, must include some means of reducing the extent of mistrust and fear on these issues. The process of negotiating an agreement which deals with these issues in a relatively formal way may be one such means.

Clients' Rights
In parallel with, but largely separate from, studies which have extended understanding of clients' views of social work has been the movement to demand more protection of the citizen's right not to be treated arbitrarily by servants of the state. This is one of the basic rights of citizenship in a democratic society but is at risk from the extensive discretionary powers which social workers can exert over their clients (Campbell, 1978).

There have been many contributions to this movement. Some cover social work generally (BASW, 1980; Barclay, 1982), others specific issues such as family involvement in decision-making, access to records and parental participation in case conferences (FSU, 1982, 1984, 1985) or the rights and a code of practice concerning people in residential care (PSSC, 1975; Centre for Policy on Ageing, 1984). The demand is towards better written rights than currently exist (NCVO, 1985). Four areas in which proposals have been made concerning clients' rights particularly interest us. As a preface to discussing these, however, we should state that, in our view, none of these rights can be regarded as absolute. Social workers often find themselves in the middle of conflicts between the rights of individuals and the responsibility of their employer to carry out obligations laid down by statute. However, these conflicts are often easier to resolve than those which develop between different individuals in the same situation. For example, by exercising a right to continue living alone at home, a mentally-infirm old person may be imposing intolerable strains on a neighbour or relative. Whose right to participate in the decision-making process is paramount here?

Clients' Rights: at the Point of Referral
The demands for more detailed information to be available to potential clients at the point of referral certainly fits the evidence from the studies of clients' views. Thus, residential establishments have been encouraged to set out their aims in a form which individuals could scrutinise before applying for admission (PSSC, 1975). Agencies are urged to ensure that the public, especially those groups most likely to need their services and new clients, are aware of what is available through the right to receive a

detailed explanation of the services the agency provides together with a statement of anything they are required to do in return and the extent to which they are entitled by law or local policy to receive this help (NCVO, 1985). Agencies should make explicit the criteria used to determine people's eligibility to a particular service as well as any need to ration resources. Social workers, when considering using statutory powers, should inform clients of their legal rights (BASW, 1980). FSU (1982) recommended that each unit should develop clear and explicit referral procedures. Some have developed explanatory brochures for families and designed referral forms for families to complete themselves or with help from a professional worker.

An alternative or addition to simple leaflets is for information to be given in initial interviews, the purpose of which is to identify any problems which can be alleviated. Then the worker offers to help the client over a longer period with the identified problems and the client is free either to end contact at this point or to enter a contract for a further sequence of interviews. This approach enables clients to make a rather more informed decision, based on some experience, about whether to participate in a change-effort (Gibbons *et al.*, 1985).

Clients' Rights: Participation in Decision-making

Although client self-determination, the right to exercise choices in the course of their involvement with social workers, has traditionally been regarded as one of the foundations of social work values, a social worker's intervention in a person's life is usually associated with a reduction in the extent to which an individual can make decisions independently (Plant, 1970; Whittington, 1971). Arguably, it is because the circumstances in which social workers enter people's lives are associated so often with significant encroachments on personal freedoms that social work sets so much store by the need to preserve what remains.

For residential provision high priority has been placed on the need to help clients retain some scope for self-determination. Thus, the decision to live in a residential establishment should be an expression of a person's individuality, as far as possible a positive choice and not a last resort. A range of options should be available to people faced with the need to accept some form of residential provision, with clients encouraged to play a part not merely in decisions relating to their own care but also in decisions about how the home is run (PSSC, 1975). The demand is for clients to have the right to be able to make their own decisions and to have real influence over those decisions they have been considered sometimes unsuitable to participate in (Page and Clark, 1977). The demand is for a general shift of power from the providers to the receivers. Where people become clients involuntarily, particular care should be taken to safeguard those rights which remain (NCVO, 1985).

Given the dangers of token efforts to improve participation, recommendations have been made that clients should be able to negotiate a contract to govern the form in which they are helped, to take part in any decision-making process involving their admission to or discharge from residential care and to be involved in case conferences considering the needs of children at risk (BASW, 1980), the onus being on the agency to show reasons why parents should not be invited (FSU, 1982, 1984). However, if contracts about aims and methods of work are to offer a fairer deal to clients (NCVO, 1985) and to involve clients more fully in decision-making, regular reviews and updates will be necessary. There is already a statutory duty to regularly review the progress of children in care. Older children and their parents or carers often attend these reviews. This could be extended to clients in residential care having the right to have and attend regular reviews (PSSC, 1975; Centre for Policy on Ageing, 1984). Clients' participation in the making of important decisions can hardly be implemented without some system of regular reviews.

However, limited experience is available to guide practitioners between the hazards of tokenism and non-involvement. It is not sufficient to allow teenagers to attend their reviews without first undertaking preparatory work to enable them to contribute effectively. Therefore, we have outlined below our agency procedures in Leeds Family Service Unit which have been designed to help clients participate in decision-making.

When a worker from another agency wishes to refer a family to our agency, we send out a referral form designed to enable families either to complete it alone or with the help of the referring worker. If a completed form is returned to us, two workers are given the task of convening two exploratory meetings with family members to ascertain how they perceive their situation and whether they acknowledge the need for any external help. The referring worker is usually invited to the first meeting to explain their concerns. At this stage we shall send the family our brochure outlining the services we can provide.

At the first meeting we explain that the family can choose whether to work with us and that we shall be deciding whether we can work with them and whether they need help from us. We then invite the family to tell us about the difficulties they are experiencing and any history they consider relevant. We usually respond by outlining the kind of help we might be able to give them in the light of what they have told us. We make notes of the discussion, written up subsequently and sent to the family. Often we shall add questions which we wish to raise. At the second meeting we usually begin by going through the notes together, asking the family to correct any inaccuracies or false impressions we might have gained. We discuss the specific questions we have identified and then ask the family whether, in principle, they wish to work with us. We also tell them what our opinions are at this stage. Notes are made of this meeting from which a report is prepared for the next staff meeting where a decision is taken whether or not to accept responsibility for the family.

Once a family is allocated to a worker the aim will be to formulate an agreement or understanding about the aims and means of the work. This will provide the framework within which the help can be given. After an interval of some months a review will be held to which the parents and older children are invited along with any workers from the unit who have been involved in the work. Workers from other agencies are invited occasionally when their help is central to any agreements we make. The review is chaired by the key worker's supervisor at the unit whose task is to ensure that the family's opinions are sought and obtained. Written reports are usually prepared in advance of the review by the workers involved. Clients have the chance to read these beforehand. The chairperson attempts to ensure that, by the end of the review, there is a revised agreement between all the people attending the meeting and writes some notes recording what was agreed. Copies are given to everyone who attended.

Our experience has been that most clients like and rarely fail to attend these meetings. It is more difficult to ensure that they participate actively in discussion and in the decisions which are made. This requires an active commitment and considerable skill from the chairperson although clients who have been well prepared or who have gone through the process before often show greater confidence.

Clients' Rights: Access to Records
Only recently has it been seriously suggested that social workers should make their records available to clients: a movement from not considering the question (PSSC, 1975) through a general rule that clients should have access to their records (BASW, 1980) to more detailed proposals (BASW, 1983; Centre for Policy on Ageing, 1984; FSU, 1985; NCVO, 1985), recommendations translated into policy in a diluted form in a circular to local authorities (DHSS, 1983).

However, opening files to clients is not necessarily a straightforward process. Some clients do not want to read their files, the knowledge that they could if they wished to being sufficient reassurance for them (Preston-Shoot, 1985). When files are kept on families rather than individuals, problems may arise if one family member confides information which he or she does not wish to confide with others. Often information is received from third parties on the understanding that their identity will not be revealed. Sometimes social workers work in environments which lack the resources to enable them to keep legible, up-to-date records. Rules or guidelines have been developed to deal with these dilemmas (FSU, 1985) but it is unlikely that guidelines can be designed to cover every eventuality. Some problems may need to be resolved by negotiation on a case-by-case basis.

The movement to open files to clients is welcome, however, as an indication of the change taking place in the nature of the client–social worker relationship. It will require social workers to develop new skills and adapt existing practices if they are to adopt an active open-records policy. It may be a key area also for attention when social workers are negotiating a contract with a client-system to guide their work together. Many of the potential dilemmas can be anticipated more easily in the context of specific clients' situations.

Clients' Rights: Appeals and Complaints
Whether living in the community or in residential care, clients have few satisfactory channels through which to complain about how they were treated or to challenge decisions made about them with which they disagree. Access to the courts or local Ombudsman is restricted to fairly narrow areas. Clients of local authority social workers can turn to local councillors who will frequently seek an explanation from senior managers but who rarely will have the knowledge or expertise to scrutinise any matter in more detail. Clients of the probation service or of social work agencies in the voluntary sector have even fewer channels through which to make representations.

It is not surprising, therefore, that recent moves to extend clients' rights and improve opportunities for client participation have led also to demands for closer scrutiny of the use of discretionary powers available to social workers and for the right of aggrieved persons to have access to some machinery for redress of grievances and to an independent professional opinion as to what constitutes acceptable practice (Barclay, 1982). It has been recommended that all agencies providing residential care should establish clear procedures for investigating complaints (PSSC, 1975) and that when complaints cannot be resolved internally the matter should be referred to the registration authority which would have the duty to investigate and adjudicate the complaint (Centre for Policy on Ageing, 1984). More detailed proposals have been made, namely that:

1. Agencies should take seriously their clients' requests to change social worker.
2. Clients should have the right to complain to someone other than the original worker about treatment which they consider 'improper or inappropriate'.
3. Proper procedures for dealing with complaints should be established and clients should be able to appeal to an independent officer if they are dissatisfied about how their complaint has been dealt with.
4. Ways should be found of setting up an independent complaints procedure for the voluntary sector (NCVO, 1985).

These recommendations interest us since a major weakness in the arguments for adopting a contractual model of practice has been the absence of any machinery for dealing with situations where social workers have failed to deliver their side of the bargain. A proper complaints procedure might provide that machinery. It is true also that in the present climate of practice a complaints authority might face difficulties because the tasks and responsibilities of social workers are defined so poorly. Contracts might provide the people investigating complaints with some benchmark against which to evaluate the service actually provided. They would indicate also whether the agency had assessed properly the client's need and whether it had been prepared to mobilise the necessary resources.

Conclusion

This chapter has reviewed the expanding state of knowledge about clients' perceptions of and experiences with social workers. The factors leading to the 'clash in perspective' have been discussed together with some proposals aimed at alleviating the problem. Some of the demands being made by various organisations and pressure groups to improve the level of participation in decisions made by social workers which affect clients have been surveyed. These demands and proposals are not in any sense radical or subversive but have emerged from working parties established by the social work profession itself and from committees set up by government.

Our thesis is that both the empirical evidence from the various consumer studies and the proposals and demands for improvements in clients' rights support the arguments for the wider and more specific use of contracts in social work. Contracts could mitigate the 'clash in perspective' and improve the level of client participation.

Note

1. The term 'unicausal–moralistic–suppressive attitude', coined by Mayer and Timms (1970) to describe the overall pattern of clients' attitudes to the problems they brought to social workers, may require translation. 'Unicausal' refers to the commonly held view that their problem had one easily identified cause (usually the conduct of their partner or some other relative). 'Moralistic' refers to the tendency of clients to see the problem in terms of blameworthy conduct: somebody had transgressed the rules or norms by which they lived and should be condemned, criticised or punished. 'Suppressive' refers to the expectation they had as to how the social worker should respond. The worker was expected to attempt to restore normality by giving the blameworthy person a piece of their mind. The social worker was seen as a means by which the unacceptable behaviour of the deviant member could be suppressed.

3 The Ingredients of a Contract

Introduction

This chapter examines the concept of contract in detail. Social work theory has always adapted ideas and models from other disciplines; here we are borrowing ideas from the concept of contract in law. The increasing use of the term 'contract' in social work has been criticised because it has a precise legal definition and most social workers operating in Britain could not meet the conditions necessary for a contract to be valid in law (Rimmer,1978). Admittedly, social workers cannot make agreements with clients which would be recognised by the courts as legally binding. However, the term 'contract' has wider meanings than those ascribed to it by legal texts, namely: agreement between parties; a business agreement for the supply of goods or performance of work at a fixed price; an accepted promise to do or forbear. Although contracts in social work cannot satisfy altogether the stringent conditions laid down by the courts, they can be improved by borrowing from the various rules and procedures evolved in contract law to ensure that the parties are fairly treated. Therefore, this chapter outlines the various ingredients of a contract in law which, in our judgement, are most relevant to social work practice. The different ways in which contracts might come to an end are considered. The major categories of defect which the law would regard as sufficiently serious to jeopardise the validity of a contract are reviewed. Actual or hypothetical examples will illustrate the main points.

Essential Features

Agreements and Binding Obligations

A contract in law is an agreement which binds the parties. It is distinguished from other agreements by the feature of binding legal obligation. What distinguishes contractual obligations from other obligations is the feature of agreement (Davies,1970). Clearly contracts which social workers might use would not normally feature 'binding legal obligation' but the substitution for that phrase of the words 'morally binding commitment' might provide a sufficient definition for our purpose. The crucial ingredient is the feature of agreement which distinguishes it from other commitments and obligations such as paying income tax, which is imposed by law, or caring for sick family members which is not imposed by law but is based on cultural traditions. Neither of these commitments includes the feature of agreement.

Relationships between social workers and their clients can and perhaps should take the form of 'agreements between parties'. Explicit contractual agreements would distinguish practitioner-client relationships from friendships and familial relationships and would emphasise that the parties have essentially different interests but have come together for a specific purpose and because the interaction offers each party an efficient means to reach their own ends (Bland and Bland,1985).

Negotiating contracts implies a process of choice, decision-making and shared commitment to realise the agreed objectives. Freedom of choice may be restricted, for example, by the absence of other facilities, but the law takes a fairly robust view of the limits to any individual's freedom of choice. For instance, it will recognise the existence of a contract between the Electricity Board and a consumer even though the consumer's choice is restricted to accepting the Board's standard terms and conditions or doing without electricity altogether. In social work, the process of exercising some choice when entering into agreements can provide a sense of purpose and commitment because the commitment is interpreted as morally binding (Liebmann,1980).

Invitation to Treat, Offer and Acceptance

Some contracts emerge after lengthy negotiations involving offer and counter-offer, hard bargaining and detailed specifications of what is involved. Others are made in an instant, as when passengers pay fares on boarding a bus. What is common is a recognisable sequence of events: an offer, the acceptance of an offer and communication of the acceptance to the party who made the offer.

Once an offer is made knowingly and intentionally it cannot be withdrawn unless certain conditions are made clear when the offer is made. For example, tradesmen may submit estimates for work at a fixed price with the condition attached that the price will be held only for a limited period. Courts will uphold a contract normally where it can be shown that an offer which was knowingly made has been accepted by the other party and where that acceptance has been communicated to the person who made the offer. Without communication the process of offer and acceptance remains incomplete. Except in some specific circumstances there is no legal requirement for a contract to be set out in writing. In many areas of economic life the need to produce a written document would obstruct the process of reaching and implementing agreements.

Where the parties already know and understand each other's interests and deal with each other regularly, the process may begin with a formal offer. A householder, wanting repairs done, may approach a firm with which they have dealt in the past and request that the work be carried out without any discussion about price or time limits. However, the householder might ask various firms to survey the problem and submit detailed specifications and estimates. This householder is not making an offer and is not bound to accept any of the estimates submitted. This stage, which may or may not lead eventually to a contract, is called an 'invitation to treat'. The parties have an opportunity to display and inspect the goods and services another party provides or needs without being committed to making or accepting an offer.

Since people often are unfamiliar with the services social work agencies provide, this preliminary stage is crucially important. We put considerable effort into the task of communicating to families the range of services we can offer. A leaflet outlines our methods of work and the unit's resources. We may show families around the unit building, describing some of the main activities which take place. At this stage we do not make an offer to work with them nor do we imply that they would wish necessarily to use all or most of the various services we provide. It is not always easy to make clear the purpose of this stage in the negotiations. Sometimes expectations are raised which cannot be met. In other cases families may be frightened off, afraid of being submerged by all the different forms in which help might be delivered.

The following example highlights the distinction between the stages of 'invitation to treat' and 'offer and acceptance'. The Jackson family were referred by a health visitor. Mrs Jackson and her youngest son were in poor health. Mrs Jackson was waiting to enter hospital for minor surgery. Mr Jackson also seemed unwell but refused to seek medical attention. The youngest child, although over two years old, had virtually no language. His four older siblings, all at school, were described as pale, wan and lacking in sparkle. The family's electricity had been disconnected for four years. A debt of £600 remained outstanding.

At the first meeting we used our leaflet to explain the kind of work we did. We highlighted particularly the playgroups for children with special needs, suggesting that either parent might like to attend these groups with their youngest son in an effort to accelerate his language acquisition.

The parents described the absence of electricity as the main problem. Mr Jackson had accepted liability for the debt and was willing to pay it off as best he could but the Electricity Board had declined to make any commitment about how much needed to be paid before they would reconnect. In desperation, he had reconnected the supply illegally once, which explained the Board's reluctance to come to any arrangement. He did not want charity but could not raise a large sum from his social security to pay off the debt.

In this first meeting we explored the kind of help the family needed and would accept. We invited them to 'treat' with us but we made no formal offers nor did we seek any commitments from them. We sensed their suspicion of social workers since several times they emphasised that they were not neglecting their children despite all their difficulties. We sought their permission to contact the Electricity Board and asked them how much they thought they could afford to pay each week out of their income. They said they could manage £10 weekly if it would lead to their supply being restored. We arranged a second meeting when we would try to decide how to address the problems.

Between meetings we contacted the Electricity Board but they would not consider reconnection until at least half the debt had been paid off. However, we succeeded in getting the Board to make a written commitment that they would reconnect if that sum was raised, a promise that they had not been prepared to give Mr Jackson. We decided to accept the family's definition of the primary problem both because of the stress which the absence of electricity created and also becuse we felt they would not accept other help unless we took this problem seriously. However, concerned about Mrs Jackson's health and the youngest boy's lack of recognisable speech, we decided to offer help in these areas too.

In the second meeting we negotiated around a number of specific proposals. Since Mr Jackson stressed his willingness to begin paying off the debt we decided to use that as part of the family's 'consideration'. In exchange, we offered to collect his payment of £10 each week and pay it into the Unit account until we had raised enough money to obtain reconnection. We made it clear that he could reclaim his money at any time and that we would return it if negotiations broke down for any reason. We offered to apply to the Social Services Committee for a grant to go towards the debt and we asked the parents to help us prepare the necessary report. We did not feel optimistic about this source of help and felt more confident that we would be able to raise some money from charitable trusts. We did not offer this because Mr Jackson was resistant to the idea of getting help from 'charity'. We kept that idea to ourselves in the hope that Mr Jackson might find it more acceptable once he had restored some of his self-respect by making a number of payments.

Both parents had been very unenthusiastic about coming to playgroups at the unit with their youngest son, so we had explored the possibility of securing a place at the local day nursery. We had been told that a priority place could be offered only with a recommendation from a paediatric assessment. We felt also that the older children needed to learn that their responses to the youngest child's cries and screams, rushing around to meet his needs, were not in his best interests and that they could be more help by encouraging him to tell them what he wanted. They had looked lethargic and under-stimulated also. We had decided, therefore, to offer them a short series of play sessions.

The parents accepted our offer concerning negotiations with the Electricity Board and agreed to pay our worker £10 weekly until reconnection had been achieved. They agreed to take their son for a paediatric assessment and to visit the day nursery with our worker to discuss whether the staff could take him and to find out what they would expect. However, they declined the offer of play sessions. They may have wished to repudiate the concealed message that the children's needs were not being met adequately already. We acknowledged their right not to accept all parts of the package we had offered.

The proposed contract was endorsed by the team and the allocated worker used the next meeting with the family to go through a draft agreement. The parents were given a copy of the final version, given below.

Agreement between Pat of Leeds FSU and Mr and Mrs Jackson

1   Areas that the work will cover

a) electricity reconnection.
   i) Pat will contact the Social Services Department to apply for a grant. This will be used as part of the lump-sum to be paid to the Electricity Board so that they will reconnect the supply.
   ii) In order to support the application for a grant, Mr and Mrs Jackson agree to help Pat write a letter giving details of their family circumstances.
   iii) Mr and Mrs Jackson agree to pay £10 weekly to the unit as part of the lump-sum needed for reconnection until we have raised enough money. Pat agrees to call at their home every week to collect this money. The unit will pay it into their bank. If the Board refuses to reconnect, the unit will return the money immediately.
   iv) When and if the Board agrees to reconnect, Mr and Mrs Jackson agree to pay the Board £9.45 weekly, to be deducted at source from their supplementary benefit. Pat agrees to contact the DHSS to arrange this.

b) a nursery place for Simon
   i) Mr and Mrs Jackson agree to apply for a day nursery place for Simon and to take him regularly.
   ii) To secure a place for Simon, Mr and Mrs Jackson agree to cooperate in obtaining a paediatric assessment on Simon. The purpose of this is to establish whether he needs a priority place.
   iii) Pat agrees to contact the paediatrician to arrange an appointment. Pat will accompany the parents and Simon to the appointment.

2. Time-limits

Mr and Mrs Jackson and Pat will work together until February. A meeting will be held then to review this work and to discuss if the family want any further help.

3. Review

If Pat or the family feel that parts of the agreement are not working out they can ask for a meeting to be arranged. John [Pat's supervisor] will chair the meeting to resolve any disagreements.

This process of negotiation began with an exploration of the nature of the problem and the parents' attitudes to the difficulties they were facing. Traditional social work skills were utilised: observation of interactions, engaging with the client, respecting their belief-systems, and developing hypotheses to explain the functional difficulties in the system. Between the two meetings we thought hard about the kind of agreement we could reach with this family. We made enquiries also of other relevant agencies about their position. The second meeting focused on an exchange of offers. The final package, influenced by the parents' preferences, was accepted by us and the family. This acceptance was communicated when the written document was exchanged.

In this case the different stages of 'invitation to treat', 'offer', 'acceptance' and 'communication of acceptance' were neatly separated into the first, second and third contacts with the family. More often they merge into one another in ways which make it difficult to maintain the important conceptual distinction between the 'invitation to treat' stage and the 'offer and acceptance' stage. In our example, the most important work was done between the first and second meetings when the workers analysed the key issues, the package which would be acceptable to the family and the position of the other agencies. The distinction between these two phases can be used deliberately. Clients can be asked to think over certain proposals or questions. Workers can use the time to reflect on the problems they have encountered, to discuss them in supervision or to consult with colleagues with special expertise. Negotiations can be begun with other agencies which may control resources essential to a resolution of the problem. Even where it is not possible to separate the phases temporally, a period of 'time-out' can be introduced to mark the boundary and reflect on what specific proposals to make.

Consideration

Consideration is essential to the concept of contract. In law, money payments, goods or services, personal actions or promises can be recognised as considerations in contracts. The courts do not consider usually whether the considerations exchanged represent fair value. However, they will rule as to whether they are sufficient. A consideration is insufficient in law if it involves:

1. Favours already granted before the bargain was struck. Thus, an agreement in which a family agreed to participate in weekly budgeting sessions *after* a social worker had negotiated a grant to pay off a fuel debt would not be a valid contract.
2. Acts or promises which they are bound by law to carry out or observe anyway. Thus, a probationer could not make a contract

with a probation officer using as consideration a promise not to drive a car without insurance since insurance is required by law.

A contract does not exist unless there is valid consideration on both sides. Social workers often find this difficult to accept. Many examples of 'contracts' are deficient in this respect either because they say nothing about any commitments from social workers in return for the clients' commitments (Rimmer,1978) or because the promises extracted from clients consist of duties which they are already obliged by law to carry out. The following example contains both deficiencies described above. It was drawn up after the Emergency Duty Team, called out twice because the children had been left unattended at night, had received the children briefly into care. A supervision order was already in existence. Consideration on the part of the social worker is absent while the consideration required of the client is insufficient. Additionally, the agreement fails to address any of the problems which had led Mrs Brown to leave the children originally. It might be argued that the agreement contains an implicit promise by Social Services to refrain from initiating care proceedings so long as Mrs Brown adheres to her side of the agreement. However, no social worker or child protection agency could make such a commitment since other circumstances might arise whereby intervention was needed even though Mrs Brown had kept all the commitments set out in this agreement.

Northlands County Council Department of Social Services

Agreement between Margaret Brown, 12 Hawthorn Road, and Jane Macmillan, Social Services Department, for the return of her children.

1. I understand that I am responsible AT ALL TIMES for the safety and care of my children.
2. I undertake NEVER to leave them alone but if I have to I will make proper arrangements for their care with another responsible adult.
3. I will make myself available to my social worker weekly or whenever requested.
4. I undertake to send my children to school regularly and cover any absences by letter or phone call.
5. I understand that if I do not keep to this agreement then, as the children are already on supervision orders, the Social Services Department can take the case back to court for care orders.

Signed .... (Margaret Brown)

.... (Jane Macmillan, Social Worker).

There must be consideration on both sides for an agreement to have contractual status. It must involve the parties in responsibilities and duties over and above those already laid down by the civil and criminal law. It must not involve the parties in illegal acts. The commitments must refer to the present and future rather than to the past. In the Jackson contract, the family's consideration included helping the social worker write a letter in support of their grant application, paying £10 weekly towards the debt and cooperating in obtaining a paediatric assessment. The social worker's consideration included applying for a grant for the family, collecting their weekly payments and arranging an appointment with a paediatrician.

Intention

Intention to contract is present only when parties to an agreement recognise its significance by their readiness to accept the consequences of non-compliance. The law assumes that parties to business contracts take the consequences of non-compliance into account when they engage in a contract. It does not make that assumption in respect of agreements made in a domestic context. Only where there is evidence that the contractual nature of an agreement was made clear to the parties at the time it was made would a court be prepared to accept such an agreement as contractual. The agreements between social workers and their clients are not clearly analogous either to business contracts or domestic agreements. They might be characterised best as a form of hybrid.

Whether intention is present in contracts negotiated between social workers and clients can be answered definitively only with hindsight. For example, an agreement between the Jones family and their social worker had included a commitment to tackle the issue of how the family treated Mrs Jones' eldest child who was in the care of the local authority. When interviewed sometime later Mr Jones said in relation to this child that he was not in his agreement even though he readily agreed that he had signed a written document which included a commitment to work on that issue (Smith and Corden, 1981). One problem, therefore, is knowing whether clients realise what they are committing themselves to when the agreement is being negotiated. When their experience is of social workers telling them what to do, the idea of negotiating an agreement about areas of work may confuse them.

To ensure that intention is present social workers must emphasise either the contractual nature of the agreement or discuss with clients the status of the agreement and agree what should happen if anybody fails to honour their part. If the concept of contract became more familiar to those involved with social workers, the difficulties of ensuring that intention is present might diminish. Meanwhile, the onus must remain on social workers to clarify the status of agreements which they negotiate and to spell out the consequences of non-compliance, for example case closure or review meetings, especially when these might be serious such as a decision to initiate care proceedings.

Ending Contracts

Contracts may be brought to an end in several ways. Ideally, all the parties realise their objectives and honour their commitments to the other participants. Wherever possible it is useful to identify some specific indicators by which it can be established whether the commitments have been honoured and the goals achieved.

However, social workers need to consider also how contracts may be terminated when some or all aspects of the original agreement remain unfulfilled. Some problems may prove to be insuperable despite the best efforts of all parties. With the Jacksons the worker might have been unable to raise any money to help them reduce their debt and reconnection, therefore, might have remained an unattainable goal. In such circumstances the parties may agree to abandon the contract, to extricate themselves and each other from unproductive interaction. No further action may be desirable or necessary, for example where a contract with a couple aimed at overcoming marital difficulties has failed to achieve any change. Or, additional work may be required, for instance where a hostel resident needs help to find alternative accommodation when the contract on which he has entered the hostel proves unworkable.

More often, contracts may need to be revised. Provided the parties agree, contracts can be revised either to integrate deeper understanding of the areas the parties want to change or to incorporate changed circumstances. What is needed is an opportunity for the parties to review the progress made on the original contract and an honest exchange of views about the areas where there has been difficulty. Is it because change is not really what one party wants or is it that the social worker's methods have been unacceptable or inappropriate? Whatever the problems, the only essential precondition to revising contracts is that the parties agree about how they should be revised.

Contract law also provides for circumstances which were not and reasonably could not have been foreseen at the time when the original contract was drawn up. Certain circumstances may be held to 'frustrate' a contract and render it irrelevant. For example, a contract with a couple to discuss tensions in their relationship would be frustrated if one party left home for good.

More difficult issues arise when one party fails to honour their side of an agreement. The law would normally regard this as breach of contract. Its remedy would be to order them to recompense the injured party. Except in special circumstances the court will not order the person in breach of contract to carry out those obligations they have failed to perform. Its intervention will be limited to restoring the position as far as possible to that which existed before the contract was agreed. The injured party has the right in law to rescind any commitments they made unless they have already gained some material advantage from the other party's performance before the contract was breached. For social workers the right of 'rescission' may be sufficient as the means for ending contracts where clients have breached them but exercising this right is unlikely to help workers reach their objectives. For clients, the absence of any obvious means of seeking restitution when they have been let down by social workers is a major weakness which will have to be remedied eventually. It seems unlikely that restitution would need often to take the form of money payments since the analogy with the legal position would require only a tribunal or complaints procedure to restore the position to that which applied before the social worker became involved. It would be unusual for clients to be financially worse off as a result of a social worker's failure to honour their side of a contract.

An illustration from our experience highlights the difficulties which arise when contracts are breached. An Education Welfare Officer had asked a family's social worker to address the problem of severe truancy presented by one of the children. The social worker agreed to do this on the understanding that she would be allowed two weeks to attempt to bring about an improvement. The EWO promised not to refer the matter to her superiors for statutory intervention in that period. When the child failed to attend school on the first morning of that period, the EWO immediately referred the case to her superiors and statutory intervention was begun. In this instance, the only remedy available to the social worker was to complain to the EWO's superior officer. It was evident that he would have been unsympathetic as he had been pressing the EWO to intervene earlier. There was also the option of withdrawing goodwill in other cases on which there might have been a common interest but this might have disadvantaged other clients and would have been unlikely to change the EWO's approach.

Defects in Contracts

One major criticism of using contracts in social work is that, whereas in law the parties are assumed to have freedom of choice, the power balance between social worker and client is so unequal that this assumption cannot be taken for granted. Statutory intervention or the threat of it, age or the client's mental state can severely diminish or erode their freedom. Additionally, social workers' professional skills in making and working through relationships will put them at an unfair advantage in any negotiations.

Once again the rules which have evolved in law to deal with analogous problems are helpful. In law some defects are so fundamental that a court would regard as void any contract which contained one. The absence of consideration or of evidence of intention are such examples. Other defects merely render contracts voidable: that is their presence gives the court power to declare a contract invalid if it considers that the defect materially affected the parties' decisions to enter the contract. Three categories of defect are worth considering here.

Duress

In law, duress is limited usually to physical violence or threats of violence. In social work, clients can experience pressures which may be as powerful as the threat of physical violence. Where clients are required to live in residential establishments against their will, for example, bail hostels or penal institutions, the pressure to accept proposals made by staff may be experienced as irresistible. The use of contracts as the basis for behaviour modification programmes in such establishments has been described as a form of 'therapeutic tyranny' (Epstein, 1975). The use of contracts in these contexts needs to be approached with particular care.

Admittedly, all residential establishments must have some rules and structure. However, unless potential residents have some real freedom of choice whether to enter or leave an establishment, whether to enter into a binding obligation, it would be wrong to regard acceptance of and compliance with those rules as their consideration in return for being 'allowed' to become or remain residents. In these circumstances the staff must drop any pretence of freedom of choice and rely on other sources of authority with which to enforce their rules.

A hypothetical illustration may help to clarify this point. Brian had been charged with several thefts from cars. Aged 19, he had only recently been released from a young offenders' institution after serving a sentence for similar offences. He had never had a job. After initially remanding Brian in custody the court indicated that it would consider granting Brian bail if he could be found a place in a bail hostel. His probation officer found a place but agreed with the warden that Brian should be accepted only if he agreed to take specific steps to find employment. Naturally Brian, desperate to leave prison, quickly agreed to these conditions which were, of course, over and above those imposed by the court in granting bail and the normal rules of the hostel. The probation officer's anxiety to get these terms agreed stemmed from his concern to help Brian avoid a further custodial sentence which seemed inevitable unless Brian could demonstrate a major change in direction.

Brian's consent to the contract which his probation officer drew up while he was in custody would have been worthless. Had his consent been sought after bail had been granted, the probation officer would have been entirely within his rights to attempt to negotiate an agreement along these lines. The mistake was to give Brian the impression that his acceptance by the bail hostel was dependent on a prior agreement with his probation officer about the steps he should take to seek work.

Incapacity

Incapacity refers to situations where it is argued that one of the parties was not in a position to exercise responsible judgement when the contract was drawn up. In such instances the courts must decide not whether the person did actually exercise responsible judgement but whether they were capable of doing so. Even where it is shown that the person was 'incapable' of exercising sound judgement, that does not necessarily render a contract void. Here the law places the onus on the other party to the agreement to show that the goods or services being exchanged are suitable to the condition and actual requirements of the 'incapable' person.

Social workers often find themselves working with clients who would be regarded in law as 'incapable' either because they are too young or because they suffer from a mental disorder, for instance the acute phase of a mental illness or the mental impairment associated with dementia. While some people are too immature or damaged to participate in any negotiations which may result in a genuine agreement, the numbers are not large nor is it usually difficult to recognise the gross damage or immaturity which would preclude participation in contract-making. There is a great danger in assuming that a large proportion of the client population is 'incapable' of exercising responsible judgement. Social workers, always self-conscious about and wary of the role of the professional 'expert' who can shoulder responsibility, should not remove responsibility from the client without very careful thought (Bland and Bland,1985).

A much larger group of people are involved with social workers for whom it is unwise to assume total competence in this area but for whom the process of contract-making and the experience of trying to implement them might be particularly useful. In these cases a greater responsibility would rest on social workers to ensure that clients were not taken advantage of, that any decisions reached were appropriate to their condition and requirements and that they were acting in the client's best interests rather than reacting to pressures from family or other systems. Elderly people 'at risk' have good and bad days. Angry adolescents can swing from being very childish to a mature acceptance of an adult perspective. Some mentally handicapped persons learn to present themselves as more responsible and competent than is really the case. Social workers should have the skills to recognise when their clients are in the best position to exercise a responsible judgement and to intervene to facilitate this. We would take the view also that, wherever possible, clients' wishes should be respected and resources provided to enable them to achieve their objectives. This would not avoid situations where practitioners have to 'do what seems best' or to choose between the opinions of different people but, in our view, there should be clear reasons, fully communicated to the client, for implementing judgements which run counter to the client's opinion.

If social workers wish to defend themselves against accusations that the contracts they negotiate in some contexts are void because of their clients' incapacity, they need to show that the contracts they have concluded are appropriate to the conditions and requirements of the 'incapable' party. Some safeguards which can be used in these circumstances are described below.

Undue Influence

This is where one party has such influence over the other that it might be regarded as inappropriate pressure. In general the law considers that individuals can resist pressure and the onus falls on the aggrieved party to show that inappropriate pressure was applied. However, certain circumstances are recognised in law to place one party in a position of dominance over the other. Such 'fiduciary relationships' include the doctor–patient and solicitor–client relationship. Where such a relationship exists the onus falls on the party in the dominant position to show that inappropriate pressure was not applied and that adequate safeguards were provided to ensure that the dominant partner did not take unfair advantage of their position.

This issue raises important, complicated questions because the intimate quality of the social worker–client relationship assumes greater significance than in many other occupations by virtue of the skill social workers are assumed to have in establishing empathy with their clients and the confidential nature of the issues they are often dealing with. However, the potential problems of 'undue influence' by social workers over their clients are not confined to circumstances where contracts are being negotiated. Some clients may be persuaded by social workers to take decisions which are not in their best interests where no attempt has been made to negotiate a contract to structure their work. Others may resist advice even where it is in their best interests as a form of protest against social workers' dominant position in their lives. On the other hand, social workers clearly do not occupy the same position, in terms of the extent to which their professional competence and autonomy is sanctioned by the community, as doctors or lawyers who can, in some circumstances, be sued for professional negligence when their judgement has been seriously at fault. Indeed, the social work profession has been at pains, especially recently, not to aspire to the status of the traditional professions. One argument for the greater use of contracts in social work has stemmed from the desire to avoid perpetuating the situation where ordinary people are encouraged to rely on the expert knowledge of the specialist to provide a solution while they abdicate from any responsibility to make that solution work.

Safeguards

The defects just described highlight the kind of situation in which it may be advisable to develop certain kinds of safeguard to prevent abuse, even though the agreements reached by social workers cannot be regarded as legally binding. Such safeguards include:

1. A cooling-off period where clients may have second thoughts about the commitments they have made and the right to withdraw from the agreement within a limited period after it takes effect. This safeguard is especially beneficial where contracts are negotiated at

times of crisis or upheaval or where the agreement which is made may create upheaval, for example when it includes admission to residential care.

2. Involving a 'client's friend' in negotiations, for example as an advocate for the client's interests when there is doubt about the client's ability to enter into any firm agreement. The advocate's task is to ensure that the agreement reached is not oppressive or exploitative. The advocate could be a friend, relative or, in residential contexts, a fellow resident. Where there is no one in the client's network who does not have a vested interest in the outcome, voluntary organisations or pressure groups such as Age Concern or Family Rights Group may be willing to accept this responsibility.

3. Escape clauses, valuable when clients may experience contracts as unreasonably demanding or intrusive. A clause which provides a legitimate 'get out' may, by its presence, make the demands more tolerable. Practitioners should consider here what their position would be if the contract was not fulfilled. It is only fair that clients should know what the outcomes might be.

However, all these safeguards depend, eventually, on the commitment of the social work profession to a code of ethics which respects and protects the rights of clients. Only if social workers see contracts as a means of increasing client power, rather than as a means of pinning down elusive people to specific commitments, will our purpose in advocating contracts as a core concept of social work theory and practice be achieved.

Conclusion

In borrowing ideas from the legal concept of contract we are not suggesting that client–social worker relationships should be re-structured to fit into a pattern more relevant to commercial and business transactions. However, some elements of this concept are desirable and inevitable and introducing contracts offers clients the potential to exercise more influence over the nature and quality of the service they are offered provided adequate safeguards are built in.

Contracts offer frameworks; they do not determine the content of the help or service which is to be provided. Practitioners should not see the concept of contracts as an alternative to the various skills and methods which have developed already to realise change or to maintain threatened stability. Indeed, the reverse is more likely to be the case as social workers may find they need to be more specific about the means by which they intend to improve problematic situations.

4 Different Types of Contract

Introduction
This chapter examines the various kinds of contract social workers may negotiate and use. Three different dimensions and two different types of clause will be presented. A distinction will be made between contracts where the practitioner is and is not a party to the agreements. Some examples will be used to illustrate this emerging typology.

The First Dimension: Involvement – Non-involvement
This dimension reflects the changing balance of dependence and independence through which social work–client relationships may pass. Four types of contract fall on this dimension which may reflect too the extent of trust or mistrust which may exist between the parties.

Preliminary Contracts
These are agreements developed to structure the process of initial negotiation, to assess whether there is a basis for further work together. They are useful where the investment of resources being proposed can be effective only with the cooperation and consent of the intended beneficiary. Residential establishments, aiming to provide a therapeutic/support service to their residents, sometimes offer a short trial period to provide a real experience of what might be involved before final decisions are made.

Preliminary contracts will often be fairly loose agreements and should always provide legitimate 'escape clauses'. When asking someone to make a major commitment, practitioners should avoid as far as possible making this a forced choice. When old people agree to enter a home for a trial period, before deciding finally whether to give up the independent life they have enjoyed in the community, the agreement covering these trial periods should reassure the old people that their homes will be maintained, and that the community services which were available before admission will be resumed if they decide not to accept the place. Similarly, preliminary agreements should not convey messages about the resources the agency can offer unless these resources can be delivered subsequently.

Preliminary agreements should be used first, wherever the other party is being asked to accept a significant intrusion into their privacy or new and very different experiences; and secondly, in situations where the initial information available to the referring agency is insufficient to determine whether help is needed or in what form it should be delivered. They are agreements to survey what is being or could be offered.

Interim Contracts

These are agreements established where some degree of mistrust or disagreement exists between the parties and normally used where one party has longer term objectives which have either not been put to the other party for fear that they will be rejected or have been rejected as inappropriate to their needs. For example, an interim agreement may evolve where the client attributes their predicament to some material, practical or financial disadvantage which they would like the social worker to redress, and the practitioner believes that there are other interpersonal or intrapsychic issues which need to be addressed also. The worker agrees to help the client tackle the material and practical issues in the hope that the experience will create a more trusting relationship in which the client can consider and work on the more threatening issues.

Obviously there are hazards in this use of interim contracts. There is the risk that the social worker will, without acknowledging it, move away from the advocate role into the therapist role and attempt to deal with the interpersonal issues under camouflage. This practice, known as 'double agenda' casework, has rightly been criticised. The second hazard is that if social workers appear to accept without question the view that the material and practical pressures are the only areas where change is needed, they risk setting up expectations amongst their users which result in their being presented only with such issues in the future. This has been named the 'welfare cycle' (Holborn,1975).

These hazards can be avoided by carefully using feedback and review. Practitioners should include a clause to the effect that, while working for the agreed objectives, they will be considering also what other factors might be contributing to the problem and, at appropriate times, feeding these back to the other party. A review should always be built into an interim contract, a point where the worker should have a good idea whether the client yet accepts to any significant degree the view that interpersonal issues may also need attention.

Mainstream Contracts

These are agreements covering the main features of work which both parties agree needs to be attempted. They will normally be based on a hypothesis or assessment concerning the origin of the difficulty, the changes which need to be achieved and the means by which they will be pursued. They may have been preceded by preliminary or interim contracts but not necessarily so. Ideally, mainstream contracts represent a substantial amount of common ground between the parties. Where this is not the case, mainstream contracts should be distinguished from interim agreements by an explicit acknowledgment of the different points of view and the nature of the compromise which has been hammered out.

Disengagement Contracts
The process of developing and sustaining trust can be difficult and clients may find working through a series of contracts a quite powerful experience. In these circumstances clients, and indeed social workers, may be understandably reluctant to end the relationship, even where the work has been successful and the objectives achieved. One means of dealing with the fears and anxieties surrounding the process of disengagement is to agree on a graduated series of steps towards fuller independence, involving some reassurances about continued or renewed access to the agency if new problems develop or old ones reappear. Where clients have passed through phases of quite high levels of dependency, a period of several months after a closing review when they can make contact if they need further help provides some reassurance that the safety-net is not immediately being removed.

It is important to identify as clearly as possible the specific fears and concerns which either party may experience when ending is being considered and to formulate a means of dealing with these specific anxieties. A vague and general reassurance that, if problems arise in the future, the client can initiate contact neither provides a convincing form of reassurance nor offers anything more than was available before the first contract was agreed. Such open-ended reassurances may also leave the agency in difficulties if a significant number of ex-clients attempt to draw on this 'blank cheque' at the same time. More specific time-limited commitments are both more realistic in terms of exercising some control over agency workloads and more convincing from the client's perspective.

The Second Dimension: Mutuality and Reciprocity
This dimension covers the extent to which aims and methods of work are mutually agreed or are reciprocally exchanged on a *quid pro quo* basis. This dimension is necessary because the purposes of social work agencies and of clients are rarely identical. Where there is complete identity of purpose a formal contract is probably unnecessary. It has been our experience too that, as the parties achieve greater understanding and trust, they are less likely to feel the need of a written document symbolising their agreement. On the other hand, contracts which involve no element of mutually agreed aims and which are based purely on the philosophy of 'you scratch my back and I'll scratch yours' are likely to be of extremely limited value and even, in the final analysis, corrosive of the integrity of all parties.

In our view contracts which would be placed at the extreme poles of this dimension are of limited use. Most contracts will contain elements which are mutually agreed and elements which involve a reciprocal exchange. It is important to be aware of the balance of mutuality and reciprocity in any contract since the balance is likely to influence the subsequent transactions between the parties. It is reasonable to expect a higher level of mutuality in contracts with the client, the primary beneficiary, than in secondary contracts which may need to be negotiated with other agencies to make the primary agreement feasible.

The Third Dimension: Primary and Secondary Contracts

Primary contracts are made with clients: people who sanction or ask for the change agent's services, who are the expected beneficiaries of service and who have a working agreement or contract with the change agent (Pincus and Minahan, 1973). However, achieving the changes agreed by the change agent and client often may involve the cooperation or mobilisation of other people or agencies. Therefore, implementing the primary contract may involve the change agent in negotiating one or more secondary agreements with the other people or systems who might have influence over the client's predicament.

Sometimes the initial primary contract established with a client may only involve a commitment to explore with other parties the possibility of a secondary agreement. One example is where the client needs help negotiating the reconnection of their fuel supply. The social worker may reach a preliminary primary agreement with the client to have exploratory discussions with the fuel board and with other agencies which might have resources to help in this objective. After the terms and conditions have been negotiated provisionally for reconnection a mainstream primary contract may be agreed then with the client and parallel secondary agreements with the other agencies. Similarly, where agencies, concerned about the quality of care being provided to children, make regular complaints to Social Services which have to be investigated, it may be necessary to obtain the client's permission to discuss with the various agencies what they regard as minimal acceptable standards and then to negotiate with the client-system about the help they need to meet these standards.

The primary contract will not always be with those whom social workers conventionally refer to as clients. A scheme set up to offer an intensive Intermediate Treatment programme for juvenile courts may need to have a preliminary primary contract with the magistrates. This might involve a commitment from them to refer offenders who satisfy certain criteria to the scheme before considering a custodial sentence. In return, the scheme's workers may commit themselves to undertaking an assessment and to exploring with the young person concerned whether they would participate in the programme. At this stage the contract with the young person will be secondary to the contract with the courts who are the real client here. By the end of the assessment process however, a primary contract should have been established with the young person which necessarily will involve secondary agreements with the court, parents and, perhaps, the offender's social worker or probation officer.

Keeping the primary and secondary contracts in reasonable harmony with each other can be the most difficult part of the social worker's task since there is likely to be considerable tension betwen agencies who see a client's functioning as disruptive and threatening and the social work agency which is attempting to 'normalise' transactions between the stigmatised client and the agencies which administer services to the community at large. Often the social worker's main task is to absorb and neutralise these tensions by helping the client and the agencies to understand better the other's point of view (Whittington, 1983).

Occasionally it may be better to identify the different perspectives and challenge them directly. These considerations have to be taken into account when deciding how the secondary contracts should be negotiated to ensure a co-ordinated response to a situation. One method is to call all the concerned agencies to a case discussion, and to seek an endorsement of the primary contract being negotiated with the client system, together with a series of secondary agreements covering the areas for which each agency is individually responsible. This approach may be helpful when all the agencies are concerned about manifestations of the same problem and/or where there is a groundswell of sympathy for the client's predicament. At the other extreme, it may be also the method of choice when the agencies have developed already extremely negative perspectives of the client-system. In these circumstances little further damage can be done by allowing these negative views to be shared, and the meeting may serve some 'cathartic' purpose which enables agency representatives then to take up a more positive stance.

In many situations, however, it is preferable for the social worker to negotiate each secondary contract separately. Where the client is coping with difficulties on several different and unrelated fronts, separate negotiations avoid the need to make public more of the client's private affairs than is necessary. Round-table meetings also run the risk of amplifying stigma once concerns about child abuse or delinquency are voiced. Information about issues which are not the responsibility of a particular agency may affect adversely the client's position with that agency.

Where social workers deal repeatedly with similar or even identical problems, they may develop standard secondary contracts with the agencies whose cooperation they need. This can make negotiating the primary contract easier. The contract with the Jackson family described in Chapter 3 was negotiated more quickly because of the workers' previous recent and successful experience in undertaking similar negotiations with the Electricity Board for other clients. However, the standard or semi-standard secondary contract also brings hazards with it. For example, social workers may find themselves abdicating from responsibility to secure the best possible deal for individual clients whose circumstances may not be identical with previous clients facing similar difficulties. Practitioners must take care also not to become too closely allied with the agency with whom the secondary agreement has been negotiated.

Framework and Substance

So far we have considered the various dimensions along which contracts may differ. Within each contract, however, there will be some parts of the agreement which set out the framework within which the work will take place and others which cover the substance or content of the work. In negotiating any agreement attention needs to be paid both to the framework and the substance.

The framework may include agreements on some or all of the following issues:

1. The reason for referral or for the client's request for assistance.
2. Agreement about the minimum requirements for work, such as who must be present, what to do if neighbours or relatives are there, whether the television should be switched off.
3. Agreed rules about communications within the work. For example, it may be necessary to include a rule that no one speaks for someone else or that nobody interrupts when someone else is speaking.
4. A statement about the clients' rights to confidentiality and any limitations to those rights.
5. Agreement about the frequency, timing and venue of contact.
6. What records should be kept and who will have access to them.
7. What steps people should take if they cannot keep an appointment.
8. How the agreement can be altered or ended if experience shows it to be unpalatable or unhelpful.
9. What steps could be taken if one or more of the parties to the agreement fails to keep their side of the bargain.

The substance of a contract may cover the following areas:

1. A statement of the agreed aims, objectives and methods or of the aims of the various parties and how these are to be pursued.
2. Details of expectations and responsibilities: of the client and of the worker.
3. What is to be focused on and priorities within the agreed foci.
4. Specific tasks: the work that is needed to achieve the aims and who is responsible for what.
5. What the social worker offers and the limits to this, especially agency constraints and the limitations imposed on the agency by other systems, for example the courts.
6. What the clients offer, emphasising the value of their making an active contribution to the change effort.
7. Changes in circumstances which would require variation, review or termination.

8. How crises will be dealt with and what will happen in the event of breakdown or of particular events within or between sessions.

Clearly a balance has to be sought between the need to cover every eventuality and the need to keep the agreement simple and comprehensible. The more complex the situation, the more difficult it may prove to keep the agreement simple and straightforward. However, the more complex the agreement, the less likely it is to be of value in bridging the 'clash in perspective' between worker and client.

Service Contracts and Contingency Contracts

It is important to recognise the distinction between these two types of contract. 'Service' contracts are agreements negotiated between social workers and clients or other agencies where the social worker is a direct party. They aim to give greater definition or sense of direction to working relationships and to specify or allocate agreed tasks.

'Contingency' contracts, developed particularly in the field of behaviour modification, are agreements made between system members as a result of therapeutic intervention. The practitioner helps others in conflict to negotiate a means of improving their interaction. For example, a contact betwen a parent and a child may set out the circumstances under which the parent may reward the child for certain changes in behaviour. They are termed 'contingency' because the implementation of promises about rewards is contingent upon specified changes in the behaviour of other parties.

'Contingency' contracts have been developed both to mediate conflict between family members and to shape new behaviours in institutional or residential contexts. We have not attempted to deal with the specific techniques of negotiating 'contingency' contracts in this book (see Fischer and Gochros, 1975; Gambrill, 1977; Sheldon, 1980; Sheldon, 1982 for detailed discussion of the uses to which 'contingency' contracts can be put).

Examples of Different Types of Contract

Example 4:1
This draft contract was illustrated in an article describing the transition of a residential assessment centre into a day assessment unit. The unit served the juvenile courts in Belfast and the primary client system at the point of assessment were the magistrates. The transition signified a move from a focus on the pathology of the child alone to a focus on the whole family. A primary contract was established with the magistrates whereby any young person, on whom an assessment was requested, would be asked together with parents whether he would agree to cooperate with the day assessment team. If he agreed in court the case was adjourned to allow the assessment to take place.

On their first visit to the unit one team member would attempt to reach an agreement with the parents along the following lines:

1. You have been asked to visit Whitefield House because of your agreement in court to allow your son/daughter to be assessed.
2. We have an obligation to submit a report at the end of the adjournment period.
3. Whilst the immediate problem seems to be the behaviour which led to your son/daughter appearing in court, this problem must in some way affect the whole family and, therefore, we will want to take an in-depth look at the whole situation.
4. To make a complete assessment it will be necessary for: your son/daughter to attend the centre every day; for your family to meet regularly with the Whitefield staff during this period.
5. If you agree to these conditions then you will have the opportunity to contribute to the assessment report and to attend the case conference. (O'Brien, 1979)

Comment   In our typology this agreement is a secondary contract, necessary to enable the unit to fulfil its primary contract with the courts. At this stage it would not be possible to claim that either the parent or the child is the expected beneficiary of the assessment process. Obviously the potential is there for negotiating further agreements towards the end of the assessment procedure with the family which, if endorsed by the court, might be to their benefit.

It is also a preliminary contract. The assessment team do not promise to change or improve things, only to take an in-depth look at the situation. The contract is quite demanding. The offender is asked to promise to attend daily while the parent is asked to commit him or herself to participate in a series of meetings with the staff. In return they are offered the opportunity to contribute to the report and to attend the case conference.

Clause 1 sets out the reasons for referral, clause 2 the Unit's obligation arising from their contract with the court. Clause 3 indicates some of the team's hypotheses and methods and their assumption that delinquent behaviour is connected somehow with, or has an effect on, relationships within the whole family. Clause 4 sets out the consideration required from the parents and the child. Clause 5 what the team can offer in return. Some areas are left unexplained, such as what would happen if the child or parent fails to attend, or how disruptive behaviour at the Unit might be dealt with. However, as a draft contract it has the virtue of simplicity and it does not offer more than, in this context, the team can deliver.

Clause 1 is concerned with 'framework'. Clauses 2 and 3 are more concerned with 'substance': the constraints on the team, the aims of the work and some clues about their approach. Clauses 4 and 5 contain elements of both framework: frequency of meetings, regularity of attendance at the unit; and substance: the expectations on the parents and the child and what the team can offer in the way of participation in the assessment process in return for the parents' cooperation. There is no assumption that the parents and the team have agreed aims and the contract is more reciprocal than mutual in character.

Example 4:2
In Chapter 3 we gave an example of an interim agreement with the Jackson family. The workers, concerned that the children appeared under-stimulated and depressed and that two family members had serious illnesses, made several offers but the parents declined everything except help with reconnection of their electricity supply and negotiation of a day nursery place. Since these objectives seemed important to the family and workers alike, the workers recommended that this should form the basis of an agreement hoping that the family might come to accept other offers of help. Indeed, when the contract was reviewed after completion of the two agreed objectives and the family offered either closure or weekly play sessions for three months, they chose the latter, demonstrating that interim agreements can help to reduce suspicion of social workers and enable clients to accept other offers of help.

Another interim agreement evolved with the Jones family. Referred to our agency by a health visitor concerned about the care of the children, the social worker had begun work without an explicit contract. The family had appeared to accept her involvement. Reginald, the father, wanted to talk about his depression but was anxious to show that this was not connected to family life. Reginald and his wife, Angela, disagreed about how involved each should be with the family's money and who should be responsible for keeping the house clean but they did agree that control of the children was difficult at mealtimes and bedtimes. Of the five children Raymond, the middle child, worried them most because he was demanding and tested them out. Reginald was concerned about the increasing arguments between him and his wife.

At this point the family, especially Angela, began to express doubts and anxieties about social work involvement. This was acknowledged as partly stemming from previous experiences with social workers. The social worker organised a review meeting at which Angela and Reginald acknowledged both the influence of past experiences with social workers and their feelings that they were not coping as well as they had previously. As the social worker did not want to put pressure on the parents to accept involvement and because it was still unclear to what extent and where the parents wanted help, an interim agreement was concluded.

1. June will meet with the whole family once a week for two months.

These meetings will include a play session with the children and an opportunity to discuss Angela and Reginald's concerns.

2. Reginald and Angela would like to use these meetings to find ways of:
   a) improving their routines at home, especially at mealtimes and bedtimes;
   b) deciding how best they can take charge of their money;
   c) improving their relationships with all the children, especially Raymond;
   d) keeping the family going when either Angela or Reginald is depressed.

3. Angela and Reginald agree to attend a playgroup with their two youngest children, Margaret and Jeremy.

4. Angela and Reginald agree that the oldest three children, Pauline, Craig and Raymond can attend a group every Wednesday evening.

5. This agreement will be reviewed after two months to see what progress has been made and whether the family want June to continue visiting or June feels that further work is needed.

6. If anyone wants to change this agreement another review meeting will be called.

Comment   The purpose of this interim contract was to define limited areas of involvement in order to help the family decide whether what the worker could offer was acceptable to them. This is a primary contract between worker and the expected beneficiary where secondary agreements would be necessary with the playgroup leader and group workers. Clauses 1, 5 and 6 mainly cover framework issues. Clauses 2, 3 and 4 are more related to substance. Although an interim agreement, there was a high degree of congruence between the aims of the worker and the parents, as spelled out in clause 2. In that sense the contract was more mutual than reciprocal even though there were other aspects of child-care about which the worker remained concerned but which were not included in the agreement at this stage.

Example 4:3
This is an example of a mainstream contract. Sandra's two children had been made the subject of care orders a year previously after they had been injured. At that time Sandra had been living with her husband and family relationships had been characterised by violence and conflict. After they had separated Sandra had been referred to our unit by Social Services to see if a programme could be devised which would enable the local authority to return the children home on trial. This contract was drawn up after a period of increased access between Sandra and the children. The proposals had been given the necessary approval by the Community Care sub-committee of the Social Services Committee.

1. The Community Care sub-committee has approved Home on Trial for John and Susan. This means that the children will be able to live at home full-time but remain the subjects of care orders. This means that the Social Services Department will continue to decide where the children live.

2. *What do we expect from Sandra?*
   a) to care for the children safely and meet their needs physically and emotionally to allow them to develop to their full potential.
   b) to cooperate with the involvement of social workers and day nursery staff.
   c) to cooperate with monthly medical checks by either the health visitor or community paediatrician.

3. *What can we provide to help?*
   a) social work help.
   b) a family aide will visit three days each week for two hours a time to help with practical matters and child-care routines and feeding patterns. This will last for three months.
   c) John can attend day nursery three days each week (Monday, Wednesday and Friday), Susan can attend day nursery every Wednesday.
   d) Access to their father, Trevor, to take place at the day nursery every Wednesday afternoon between 2 and 4p.m.
   e) A dance and movement group every Wednesday morning at the day nursery for Sandra and John.

4. *The Future*
   a) John and Susan to remain with Sandra and in the long term to consider going back to court to discharge the care orders.
   b) Our main priority is the children and they would be removed again if:
      (i) there was reasonable cause to believe that they were being ill-treated or neglected or
      (ii) Trevor returned to live at the home.

Comment   Clause 1 is the framework: the context of the interaction between the participants and an outline of the obligations on the social worker. Clause 2 adds to the framework by specifying the social worker's expectations of the client. It introduces also the substance of the contract: what the client is responsible for to achieve the aim of enabling the children to live at home. Parts b and c of this clause require secondary agreements with the other professionals mentioned and also represent the client's consideration: personal actions or promises in the contract. Clause 3 is again substance, this time what the social worker and other agencies are offering, their consideration within the agreement. Part a is, in our view, not sufficiently specific. Parts b–e all require secondary agreements with these parties. Clause 4 contains additional substance, a restatement of the agreed aim and 'what if' clauses, changes in circumstances which would require review or variation.

In our opinion this contract could have been strengthened if it contained clauses referring to what action would be taken if the mother or social worker did not fulfil the expectations placed on them and if the children did not thrive. Additionally, the agreement could have specified what sections within it were seen as mandatory, resulting in action if they were not fulfilled, and which clauses were optional and open to the client to accept or reject. This would require the social worker to be clear, for instance, whether the dance and movement group and attendance at the clinics were essential components to the rehabilitation plan, with thought being given to removing the children if these clauses were not fulfilled.

Example 4:4

Here the social worker had recently taken over the family from a colleague who had left the Unit. Christine was a single parent who had been very isolated from family and community networks and experienced considerable anxiety about whether she was dealing appropriately with her two children. The children sensed that she did not feel confident with them and this influenced their behaviour. The worker was being encouraged also by her supervisor to work towards closure. The agreement set out below was a primary service agreement which had both 'mainstream' and 'disengagement' features. In most respects there was a high degree of agreement about aims but Christine was at best somewhat ambivalent about the proposal to reduce her involvement with the unit. In relation to the proposals for closure, therefore, the contract involved an element of reciprocity.

1. *What Christine wants to change.*
   a) Christine wants to move closer to her son, Nicholas. To bring about this change, Christine will spend one hour each weekday evening helping him with his school work.
   b) Christine wants to be a friend to her children, Nicholas and Sarah, to relax and enjoy being with them. To achieve this, Christine will do a specific activity with them as a family every Sunday afternoon. Christine can borrow toys from the Toy Library to play together as a family.
   c) Christine wants Nicholas and Sarah to play together better and to have less 'bickering'. Christine wants Nicholas to share more with Sarah. To achieve this change, Christine will follow what is described in b) above.
   d) Christine wants Nicholas to have more confidence. To achieve this change, Christine will ask Nicholas if he would like to join a group. If he wants this, Joan will help Christine to arrange this.
   e) Christine wants Sarah to have more confidence and be more independent. Joan will put Sarah's name forward for a nursery place. When one is available, Sarah will attend.
   f) Christine wants help with her writing and spelling. Joan will find

out information about Adult Education courses and help
Christine to join one.

g) Christine wants to have more confidence in herself and not to
worry so much about how other people see her. To bring about
this change Christine can join an Adult Education course and
attend a social group held each Tuesday at the office. Joan will
accompany her to two sessions.

2. *Why Joan is working with Christine.*
   a) to help Christine to bring about the above changes and not to get
   discouraged if nothing seems to be changing.
   b) to help Christine to consider and meet the needs of Nicholas,
   Sarah and herself.
   c) to help Christine to cope with being a single, working parent.

3. *Contact with Joan*

In order to help bring about the above, Christine and Joan agree to meet
once a week for two months after which they will meet once a fortnight
for a further month. After this Christine will be able to contact Joan by
telephone to make an appointment if and when she feels this necessary.

Meetings will be held at the office on Monday from 9.30 to 11. If either
Joan or Christine cannot keep an appointment, they will let the other
know as soon as possible and arrange an alternative time.

If either Joan or Christine wants to change or add to this agreement
they can do so provided the other person agrees. A review will be held
after four months to see if anything has changed and if either Joan or
Christine feels further work is needed or wanted.

Comment   Section 1 is the substance of the agreement, a statement of
objectives and specific tasks aimed at achieving the goals. Some of the
clauses involve an offer by the social worker accepted by the client and
the section involves consideration on both sides: responsibilities and
duties or commitments.

Section 2 summarises the substance of the agreement by outlining the
broad aims which have been teased out in section 1 into more specific
objectives. Section 3 is the framework of the agreement, detailing
venue, frequency of contact, the duration of the agreement and the date
for review, renegotiation or termination.

Example 4:5

Earlier in the chapter we referred to the importance of secondary
contracts: agreements between the parties to the primary contract and
other agencies or significant persons, whose cooperation is required if
the goals of the primary contract are to be achieved. This requires that
the main parties discuss their objectives with these systems and obtain
agreements which allow them to enter into their primary agreement. We
discussed the relative merits of two different strategies: the case
discussion approach and the separate negotiation process.

Once the discussions have been concluded there are again two possible approaches. All the agreements can be included within a single contract or, alternatively, separate contracts can be composed with each of the parties involved. A hypothetical example of the first approach was developed in a workshop on the use of contracts. This concerned a fourteen year old who, two years previously, was made the subject of a care order for non-school attendance. Since that time he had attended school regularly and made sufficient progress for his year tutor to feel that he should be encouraged to enter some state examinations. Michael had begun to express a wish to return home. The social worker's supervisor and the officer-in-charge of the small group home had supported this impetus, worried that Michael could stagnate in care and lose contact with his family and local community. The agreement, entered into prior to Michael returning home, involved discussions with Michael, his mother and step-father, the school, education welfare officer and residential social worker. The other interesting feature of this agreement is that it is both an example of a service contract, in which services were offered by a social worker and other professionals to achieve specific objectives; and of a contingency contract where undertakings between members of the client system were outlined in the first four clauses of the section headed Ways and Means.

Contract: Agreement between Michael Brown and Julia Hodges representing the Social Services Department.

Introduction: Michael is the subject of a Care Order made following a period of prolonged non-school attendance. This agreement has been drawn up after discussions between Michael, his social worker, Mrs Smith of the children's home, Michael's year tutor at school and his education welfare officer, and his parents.

Agreed aims:
1. To enable Michael to return home and demonstrate that he is now able to attend school regularly.
2. If the plan works and Michael does attend school regularly, to apply to the Juvenile Court for the discharge of Michael's Care Order.
3. If the court agrees to the discharge of Michael's Care Order, to support his application to join the army.

Ways and means:
1. Michael accepts responsibility for getting himself up and getting to school before 9 a.m. each day.
2. Mrs Brown has promised to buy Michael a clock-radio with a loud alarm to help him wake up in the morning. Julia will apply to the Social Services Department for a grant to cover half the cost.
3. Michael agrees to be in the house by 10 p.m. on each weekday and on Sunday nights during school term. Mrs Brown agrees to ensure that Michael is in bed by 11 p.m.
4. Mr Jones, Michael's step-father, agrees that he will leave the main responsibility for laying down the law with Michael to Mrs Brown. He

will support her when she puts her foot down.

5. Julia will visit the home each week on Wednesday at 3.30 p.m. except when she is on leave or off sick. She will discuss with Mrs Brown how the agreement is working and will also see Michael when he comes home from school to hear his point of view. If Mrs Brown or Michael is unhappy, Julia will try to help them sort out an acceptable arrangement.

6. The education welfare officer will collect the attendance record card for Michael each week and will let Julia know as soon as there are any unexplained absences.

7. Michael's year tutor agrees that the normal punishments for lateness or unexplained absence will be suspended in Michael's case for three months until it has become clear whether Michael can handle this responsibility. Instead, Michael should report to his office if he is late for school or on returning to school after any absence. After three months the normal school rules will apply to Michael.

8. Julia undertakes to find out what rules the Army Recruiting Office are now applying to applicants who have been subject to Care Orders. She will also locate the nearest Army Cadet Force and find out how Michael could join. The Social Services Department agree to pay the costs of attending while Michael is subject to a Care Order.

Ifs and buts

1. This arrangement will be reviewed after six months at a meeting to which all the parties will be invited.

2. An earlier meeting can be convened at the request of Michael, Mrs Brown or Julia if things are not working out or if there are any major changes in the situation which affect the agreement.

3. If Michael does not establish regular school attendance from home, the Social Services Department reserves the right to return him to care at once and then to convene a meeting. To minimise the disruption a place will be kept for Michael at Mrs Smith's children's home for at least four weeks after he returns home. Mrs Smith agrees not to reallocate that place until she has checked with Julia that Michael is doing well at home.

Comment   The introduction and the section entitled 'Ifs and buts' form the framework of the agreement. The remainder forms the substance. This involves offers from the various professionals, accepted by Michael and his family, and considerations: services, personal actions and promises over and above those laid down by the civil and criminal law.

Example 4:6
An example of the second approach is taken from another place of work undertaken in our own agency. In this case separate agreements were negotiated following a review of a primary, service contract. This had been negotiated originally following a case conference convened

because of non-school attendance and concern about the care received by the children. The primary contract, between Michelle (mother) and David (social worker), ran as follows:

The aims
a) to help Michelle meet the needs of all her children and to establish reasonable boundaries of behaviour and control.
b) to establish a pattern of working between Michelle and David whereby outside agencies may be satisfied that the children are being adequately cared for and protected without Michelle feeling that all her privacy is being violated. Also to establish a basis of mutual trust between Michelle and David.

The following clauses reflect areas of concern expressed at the case conference. Michelle agrees to notify and discuss with David when any of the following occur:
1. Significant accidents or injuries to any of the children.
2. Absences from school by any of the children.
3. Any intention by or for any of the children to spend substantial periods of time in the care of adults other than Michelle and in particular overnight stays.
4. The taking up of residence in the house of other adults.
5. Major problems with the behaviour of the children.

Method of work
a) Michelle and David will meet weekly at the office, alone, to discuss issues relating to the children. If either person wishes to cancel the meeting they should notify the other.
b) David will continue to visit Andrew and Paul at their school and will liaise regularly with the other schools.
c) The children will be considered where appropriate for groups and playschemes to help boost their social skills.
d) David will hold activity-based sessions with all five children fortnightly at the office.

If Michelle fails to keep to these arrangements David will either:
1. notify the divisional review of the Social Services Department or
2. reconvene the case conference (this would be in the event of serious incidents coming to his notice).

If Michelle wishes to change the above arrangements, she may ask for a review to be called where this would be discussed. In any case we will review the contract in six months time.

When this contract was reviewed after six months Michelle had adhered to the terms of the agreement, the children's school attendance had improved, and the activity-based sessions with the children had improved the relationship between them and Michelle to the point where she felt more able to control them. Neither David nor Michelle felt it appropriate to apply for the children's names to be removed from the At Risk register at this stage, but they did agree that Michelle's request for a three-month period, where she would continue to adhere to clauses 1-5 of the original contract but only meet with David if she requested this or if David felt he had to respond to concerns received from other agencies, should be supported. However, this required the agreement of the schools and the Social Services Department. The primary contract was revised once the permission of the Social Services Department had been obtained to enter into the agreement. The original aims and the five clauses previously agreed by Michelle were retained and the following clauses added:

a) David will visit Michelle in the next three months if she contacts David to request a meeting or if David receives renewed concerns from the schools or believes that Michelle has not kept to the five clauses.
b) After three months David will contact the schools for information about the children's school attendance, behaviour and progress. A review will then be held at which David and Michelle will decide whether a request can be made for the children's names to be removed from the At Risk register and whether further work is needed.

This revised agreement required that a secondary contract was negotiated with the schools. David met with the teachers concerned and agreed the following:

Background. Since the case conference none of the children has received injuries and their school attendance and behaviour have improved. It has been decided that David will only visit in the next three months if asked by the family or if the schools report concerns about attendance or performance and behaviour. Thus:
a) the teachers agree to inform David immediately of any un-explained absences from school or of any behaviour which gives cause for renewed concern.
b) if the teachers contact David he will inform Michelle im-mediately of these renewed concerns and then notify the teachers of what has been decided with Michelle.
c) if no concerns are reported to David, he will contact the schools after three months for a report on each of the children prior to a review at which decisions will be made concerning whether further social work involvement is necessary. David will invite the teachers to attend this meeting.

Example 4:7
It is not always possible to work with clients on the basis of mutually agreed objectives. For example, in Intermediate Treatment, group workers may be concerned with preventing an adolescent from committing further offences when this may not be the adolescent's

priority or reason for attending the group. In work with families it is not uncommon for parents to request assistance with rehousing or with improving the behaviour of the children. However, the social worker might identify the need for intervention as centred on improving the relationships within the family as a whole, seeing the meaning of the children's behaviour and complaints about this as originating in dysfunctional modes of relating or in dynamics between family members. Here we give one example of a reciprocal agreement negotiated with the Beer family: the mother, Caroline, and her two boys, Christopher and Charles. Initially Caroline had asked for help in controlling Christopher but this had not prevented a further deterioration in their relationship and, when Caroline asked that he be removed, a place of safety order was obtained on the grounds that he was beyond her control. In the meetings which followed, Caroline asked for help with a housing transfer and for Christopher's immediate return home, with a treatment programme for Christopher alone to 'sort him out'. The social worker, believing that a housing transfer would further unsettle Christopher and that his immediate return home would result in another breakdown of relationships, especially because Christopher was saying that he did not want to return home immediately, wanted to arrange a rehabilitation programme of family sessions and weekend leave prior to any decision about Christopher's future. The following agreement was negotiated. This is also an example both of a service and a contingency contract where the latter is a set of undertakings between members of the client system.

1. Ruth [social worker] believes that Christopher cannot return home until Ruth is certain that this would be in his best interests. She will feel this to be the case when Christopher expresses the firm belief that he wants to return home and that Caroline will both control him and care for him. Also when Caroline is able to meet his needs physically and emotionally, that is when she feels able not to reject him when he is difficult to control, and feels able to make positive efforts at understanding his view and making contact with him.
2. Caroline would like Christopher to be returned immediately but recognises that, if she were to contest the Interim Care Orders, Ruth would be unable to support her.
3. Caroline would like Christopher to receive help from Ruth. Ruth believes that some individual sessions with Christopher are appropriate and these will be held weekly. Ruth will help Christopher to work through his feelings about Caroline's request that he be taken into care and his knowledge that she did not want custody of either Christopher or Charles at the time of her divorce from her husband. However, Ruth also believes that before Christopher can return home permanently, the relationship between him and Caroline needs to be improved.
4. Caroline agrees to accept Ruth's offer of a family meeting each week

when, through activities, they will attempt to enable Caroline and Christopher to talk together, understand each other and improve their relationship.

5. Caroline agrees to visit Christopher once a week at the children's home for two hours. This will be every Wednesday. She agrees to let him know if she is unable to go.

6. Caroline agrees to collect Christopher every Friday for weekend leave and to return him on Sunday evening. Christopher agrees not to run away but to discuss his feelings about leave with Ruth and Caroline in their weekly meetings. If Christopher does not want to go home at the weekends, this must be discussed in the weekly meetings.

7. Caroline has asked Ruth to help her obtain a housing transfer. Ruth agrees to contact the Housing Office to ascertain when such a transfer will be possible.

8. This agreement will be reviewed monthly prior to each court hearing.

Conclusion

This chapter has described the various types of contracts which can be negotiated. We believe that good practice stems from planning, a systematic approach and specificity concerning who the contract is with, what the problem or situation is, what the purpose of intervention is, what change is being sought and what the roles of the various participants are. Primary and secondary agreements will founder if these basics are misunderstood. Additionally, the type of agreement entered into will depend on the extent of common ground between the parties and the stage these participants have reached in their relationship. Clearly, therefore, some clauses will remain vague until the social worker and family or group know what they want and where the change effort is to be directed. Equally, the content of the type of agreement negotiated will depend on whether the methods to be used are those of task-centred casework, family therapy or behaviour modification.

A whole range of social work skills is required during the process of clarifying what work is to be undertaken, concluding and reviewing a contract. Subsequent chapters will discuss these skills within a model for practice.

5 Contracts in Residential Work and Groupwork

Introduction

The working concept of contract is not tied specifically to any one social work method or setting. It is, therefore, a valuable bridging concept which can be applied equally well to individual counselling techniques, family therapy strategies, task-centred methods, behaviour modification, or to the task of coordinating a package of resources. The concept provides a common base of understanding for case workers and group workers and it can cross the much wider divide between residential and community-based social work. Nevertheless, the value of the concept in offering this area of common ground should not camouflage the differences which will continue to exist between the various contexts in which social work is practised. In this chapter, therefore, we attempt to address some of the points which should be considered when contracts are used in residential work or in groupwork.

We have chosen this focus because of the importance we attach to good practice in these areas. Residential social work traditionally has been the poor relation in the development of social work in Britain, yet residential workers find themselves dealing with people whom field social workers have been unable to sustain in the community. Recently, some gradual steps have been taken to bridge the gulf between residential and community-based social work and, in our view, the concept of contract has as much validity in residential settings as in work with families in the community. We are conscious also of the potential for positive change which, although largely untapped, is still available in the skilled running of groups by social workers. The relevance of the concept was acknowledged rather earlier by writers on groupwork practice than by authors who were promoting models of individual or family-based change. (Garvin, 1969).

Issues in Residential Work

Clients in residential care are, generally, more vulnerable physically and/or emotionally than people who are able to maintain some degree of independent life in the community. This vulnerability usually provides the underlying basis for their admission and is an ingredient in most of the issues which need special attention when the use of contracts in residential work is considered. These issues, which distinguish contract-making in residential work from the applications of the same model in community-based social work, may lead practitioners to doubt the value and feasibility of using contracts in residential care. However, in our view, these issues strongly point to the need for the use of this concept.

Physical Care

Common to most forms of residential work is the need to provide a high level of basic physical care for the residents. Sometimes this can be the predominant ingredient of the work. However, because the pattern of physical care is constant and repetitive, it is much easier to provide it in a mechanistic and routinised way. Individuals who have 'special' needs, or who want to be treated differently, disrupt the routine. The need for routine threatens what remains of resident individuality. Moreover, in settings where residents cannot do a great deal for themselves, due to their physical or mental infirmity, the constant provision of physical care may lead to a high level of dependency on the staff. The security of having one's basic physical needs met without effort can be extremely destructive, especially where the long-term goal is for the resident to return to a more independent life-style in the wider community.

On the credit side, the need to provide physical care does provide opportunities, which the use of contracts can enhance, rarely available to social workers in the community. Through the natural, everyday tasks of washing, feeding, cooking and housework, it is possible to engage residents in ways that provide valuable opportunities for social learning and corrective emotional experiences.

Emotional Dependence

Since most people in residential care are extremely vulnerable and because many are relatively passive recipients of physical care, they are liable to develop high levels of emotional dependence on staff. Some of the factors involved in the maintenance of this dynamic were described in Chapter 1. The structure on which the provision of residential care is based seems peculiarly ill-equipped to meet such high levels of emotional dependence: societal trends have eroded the value placed on vocational dedication, and the low status accorded to residential work has led to demands for clear and limited hours of work to protect staff from over-exposure to the stresses of residential work. Both these trends have contibuted to the demise of the 'family model' of residential care. Whether this should be regretted is an open question, one's view depending on one's confidence in the models which are replacing it. In our view, the changes are to be welcomed in that they have created a 'window of opportunity' for a different philosophy to evolve. However, we are concerned that many workers in residential settings currently appear to be working in a theoretical vacuum insofar as the task of coping with the high levels of emotional dependence is concerned.

Control of Deviant Behaviour

Many residents are admitted because their behaviour in the community could not be contained within societal norms. Gathering together a number of people, all of whom have found the restrictions of authority irksome or intolerable, inevitably creates anxiety. Often this anxiety provokes staff to respond with safety manoeuvres.

Any individual's behaviour is normally kept within bounds by the fear of losing the love and respect of people whose relationship is valued. This control is often absent in residential work and staff find they have to rely instead on the use of a tariff of rewards and privileges which may be earned by good behaviour or lost as a result of transgression of the rules. There may be a tendency to forestall trouble by clamping down on potential conflicts before they appear. These safety manoeuvres may restrict the opportunities for residents to learn self-control and to deal directly with their feelings of anger and destruction.

Those who enter residential care against their will may come to perceive the staff as the obstacle to regaining their personal freedom. In these situations, the residents may see the interests and objectives of the staff as very different from, and even alien to their own. Their feelings of anger and hostility, which in many cases will have contributed to the need for them to be admitted, may provoke staff to maintain a substantial degree of 'emotional distance' from them. Repeated exposure to outbursts of anger when one is trying to convey a message of care and concern is highly stressful. Disengagement is an understandable reaction, to which residents may respond by behaving in even more outrageous ways since this has been the pattern of their interactions for a long time prior to admission.

However, the high profile of the issue of control in some residential settings can be turned to advantage. It is possible to place some responsibility for the control of deviant behaviour upon the resident community. By involving them in the processes of making and enforcing the rules, the polarisation between staff and residents can sometimes be alleviated. It offers also opportunities for learning social skills, for negotiating and for participating in the process of shared decision-making.

The Conflict between Individual and Community
Throughout the book, we have emphasised that using contracts or specific agreements in social work helps to ensure respect for the expressed needs of each individual or family. Social workers in the community can afford usually to negotiate agreements with their clients without worrying too much about the risks that action resulting from their agreements will have damaging effects on other clients. Nor is it often likely that different clients will compare each other's contracts and then complain about inequitable treatment. These luxuries are not available to residential social workers. If one resident is allowed to keep alcohol in their room, others may demand the same right. If one old person is given permission to bring their cat into an old people's home,

another will want to bring their pet. These demands, which may be entirely reasonable in isolation, may be incompatible with each other, or they may offer more freedom than a few of the residents can cope with.

The risk is that a system of rules or restrictions evolves which is based on the lowest common denominator: that is, the level of freedom and responsibility which the least able resident can cope with. Obviously this is an unsatisfactory resolution of the conflict. Instead, workers need to establish how much in the way of individual differences their community can tolerate. It may be necessary to negotiate agreements on some issues with all the residents collectively, and to develop agreements on individual objectives and needs separately but within the framework of the collective contract.

Permanent Home or Transitional Community
An area of potential conflict, inherent in residential social work, is that which develops between the concept of providing a permanent or semi-permanent home for residents and that of providing a temporary refuge within which they can acquire the new skills or confidence necessary to return to the community. If the establishment is viewed primarily as the residents' permanent home, it will be unreasonable usually to expect them to enter into commitments to achieve personal change as a condition of continued residence. It may still be appropriate to offer them the opportunity to embark on such change, and to provide the necessary support and expertise, but not as a condition of residence. On the other hand, if the establishment is offering a form of transitional care, there is an obligation on the workers to keep in mind the need to prepare for and work towards the time when less intensive help and support will be offered. For these establishments, admission and continued residence will be contingent normally upon the client's willingness to participate in a programme of work aimed at developing or restoring skills and confidence in the various aspects of independent living.

The most difficult problems for staff arise when their establishment attempts to provide a permanent home for some residents and to offer transitional care only for others, or where the staff or management are unclear which function they are aiming to fulfil. Most difficult of all, perhaps, are the situations where the staff think they are working to re-establish residents in the community, while residents think they are being encouraged to regard the establishment as their permanent home (or vice versa). An 'organisational model' of residential care (Miller and Gwynne, 1975) offers some means of tolerating wide differences of individual need within one establishment, but staff and residents need to be clear about their aims and the overall purpose of their setting. Agreements about the terms and conditions of admission and continued residence should, wherever possible, be negotiated separately from contracts governing work of a therapeutic or social learning nature.

Incapacity

In Chapter 3 issues were discussed concerning the extent to which contracts can be negotiated with people who have very limited abilities. Attention was drawn to the guidelines evolved in contract law to deal with this problem. The issue has been addressed also elsewhere in respect of old people in residential care (Bland and Bland, 1985). Some discussion is needed here because the issue is much more to the forefront in residential work than in any other form of social work.

Two specific problems face residential workers in this area. First, in some residential settings, the very need for admission is based not only on an acknowledgement of present incapacity, but also on a realistic expectation of increasing impairment. This is true particularly of elderly mentally infirm clients and of people suffering from chronic degenerative disease. Even if it seems feasible and useful to negotiate a specific agreement when a client is first admitted, the worker will be aware that, in the future, the resident may have no memory or understanding of the process. The temptation, then, is to dismiss the exercise as futile.

The second problem is connected with the precautions which are recommended in negotiating contracts with clients where there is an element of incapacity. The worker is expected only to negotiate agreements which would generally be recognised as suitable to the condition and actual requirements of the 'incapable' person. The social worker in the community is reasonably placed to take a detached or objective view of the actual requirements of the 'incapable' person. The residential worker, on the other hand, is required to work, and sometimes live, alongside the 'incapable' person on a daily basis over a period of months or years. Inevitably, the worker is liable to become more 'enmeshed' so that, although they may have developed a much fuller appreciation of the client's potential and limitations than the field social worker, they may find it harder to take up a more detached stance.

However, neither of these problems should be seen as insurmountable. As a person's incapacity increases, they may have a much more restricted view of what is important in the quality of their life. The wish to prepare their own meals, at their own pace, may become much less important than ensuring that the meal provided for them is of a kind they find appetising and acceptable. It will rarely mean that they wish to abdicate from any influence over the form their daily life takes. The need to avoid becoming too 'enmeshed' is one which the residential worker, in particular, needs to pay attention to. This can be achieved with the help of proper supervision and consultation.

Example 5:1 Improving Communication in a Children's Home
The Larches, a community home based in the suburbs of a large town, caters for teenage children. Some have been in care for several years, their placements in foster-care or other children's homes having broken

down; others have come straight from home after being rejected by parents and behaving in ways which indicated they were beyond parental control. There are places for fifteen children. At the time of this initiative there were only eight children.

A new member of staff felt unhappy about the situation in the home. The care staff and the children spent very little time together. The care staff occupied themselves with domestic and practical tasks even though there were other staff employed to do much of this work. The children spent a great deal of time either out of the home, associating with friends in the neighbourhood, or in the 'disco room', a large room which had separate access to the outside community from the main entrance. Often they would bring their friends into the 'disco room' but staff hardly ever entered it. When they did, they were met by an atmosphere of sullen hostility which did not encourage them to stay. In their activities outside the home, some of the children were clearly placing themselves at risk. They were aged between thirteen and sixteen years. On Saturday nights, for example, they could be found in the vicinity of the local pub, being bought drinks by older boys. On some occasions this had led to sexual activity after the drinking. Staff were aware of this behaviour but chose not to confront it directly.

To the outsider coming in to work in this system, it seemed that the staff group and the resident group were colluding to maintain a situation in which communication between them was restricted to: giving permissions for staying out late or going home for weekends; getting pocket-money and buying clothes; and obtaining access to cigarettes. After some weeks of increasing discomfort, the new worker explained her feelings to the staff group. They accepted her diagnosis but expressed pessimism about the prospect of achieving any change. The new worker proposed that, with the support of the other staff, she would hold a series of children's meetings, to be attended by all the residents and those staff on duty. Her aim was to breach the barriers which had been erected between the two sub-systems of this children's home.

It was anticipated that this proposal would encounter quite powerful resistance from the children's group, especially from the teenage boys. Rather than offer it on a 'take it or leave it' basis, the new worker realised that the children could not make an informed decision about whether to participate without experiencing what might be involved. She decided to use her authority to insist that all the children come to the first meeting. She obtained the support of the staff group.

All the children were present when the first meeting began, except one whose whereabouts were unknown. As they waited for her to arrive, the anxiety level amongst the children got quite high. Eventually, the worker decided not to wait for the absent member and explained why she had called the meeting. She said that, in her experience, many children in care grew up with a lot of disadvantages: by the time they were 17 or 18 they would be expected to look after themselves, and many of them could not expect much support from their families. To cope with this, she said, they would need to develop a lot more confidence, to be able to speak for themselves, and to learn how to give each other support and how to accept help. She was suggesting that they could begin by having a meeting each week, to get used to talking about problems and worries, and so they could start taking some responsibility for themselves and having some influence over how the home was run.

At this point, one boy indicated that he wanted nothing to do with the idea. He left by a window. For a minute, it seemed as if the proposal would be rejected out of hand, but some of the others were embarrassed by his behaviour and started asking questions. How long would the meetings last? What would they talk about? The worker had stuck some newsprint on the wall and had brought some felt-tip pens. When asked what this was for, the worker said that she wanted them to brainstorm their feelings about school: what was good and what was bad about it, and what they got out of truanting (which was a chronic problem in the home at that time). This exercise got everyone involved. A lot of feelings and opinions were aired. The staff listened to the children's feelings about school: being picked on and stigmatised by other children and some teachers because they were in care. They did not pass judgement.

The worker then asked the children what they thought they could do to improve the 'disco room'. A series of ideas were proposed for redecoration and the acquisition of new equipment. Staff indicated that they would be prepared to try to obtain the materials and to help the children redecorate it and make it a nice room again, but that they would expect some cooperation from the children in accepting a greater degree of responsibility for their own behaviour. The worker then ended the meeting by getting both the staff and the children to play a simple trust game.

The meeting had provided a positive experience for most of the residents, and a novel one for the staff in that they were beginning to hear and respond to the children's opinions and feelings. The next meeting provided an opportunity for the new worker to raise an issue involving the theft of money from another staff member. The girls responded by complaining about the boys' habits of walking into their bedrooms and sometimes stealing minor possessions and valuables. They asked that locks be fitted to keep the boys out. Another request was for individualised mugs for each person. The 'disco room' was gradually being redecorated and this activity had provided staff with a reason to re-enter this forbidden territory.

From these foundations, children's meetings gradually became accepted as a regular part of the life of the home. Children admitted subsequently accepted them as part of the ethos of the home. No written agreement was developed to govern the meetings but a clear understanding evolved from the initial experience. The essential basis of the initial contract was that the meetings were intended to provide the children with a learning experience to prepare them for leaving care. This was offered in return for the children being prepared to attend the meetings and to cooperate in the effort to re-establish communication with the staff. The initial meetings provided experiences in which the children were able to raise specific issues and get a positive response. They also provided staff with the opportunity to challenge the resident group openly on issues involving unacceptable behaviour: residents had to decide whether to collude with and cover up for the deviant members or dissociate themselves from their actions.

This initiative on the part of one worker was the first tentative step towards the introduction of a contract model in a community home for adolescent children whose reason for being there, in most cases, was their record of highly disruptive behaviour. These meetings established a preliminary contract to explore the potential of regular meetings as a forum for the exchange of views, as a means by which residents could participate in the way the home was run, and as an opportunity for staff to challenge the more extreme forms of inappropriate behaviour in the resident group: individual residents would have to decide whether to accept some responsibility for keeping their own and their peers' behaviour within bounds or to continue colluding with and covering up for behaviour which many of them found unacceptable.

Example 5:2 Contracts in a Residential Home for Old People
Chancellor House is a local authority home for old people in which the use of explicit agreements at all levels has become a cornerstone of their practice, and in which staff are committed to preserving, so far as possible, the right of each resident to personal independence, personal choice, and personal responsibility for their own actions. Residents live in small bungalows designed to enable them to maintain as much independence as possible in the way they live.

The contracts between residents and staff are made up of three layers. The home produces a brochure which is given to all old people who have been put forward as possibly needing admission. This contains a series of statements about the rights and responsibilities of both residents and staff which form the first layer of the agreement: a layer which is common to all residents. Basic rights are spelled out, and the way these rights are applied to specific issues such as rules and routines, visiting, belongings and making complaints. The essence of this layer of the contract, however, is contained in the sections headed: 'What we expect of you' and 'What you can expect of us'. The first section reads:

'Our policy is to help you help yourself: We therefore expect you to do as much for yourself as possible. We will help you do things you thought were impossible!'

In the second section, the brochure lists some specific considerations offered by the staff in return for the commitment by the residents to do as much as possible for themselves:

> 'The staff will help you with tasks you are unable to cope with . . . We will help you to arrange any activities or hobbies that interest you . . . Chiropody, library and telephone facilities are also available . . . If you want a daily newspaper, you can arrange for delivery from the local newsagent just as you did in your own home.
> Should you wish to do your own personal laundry, facilities are provided.
> No member of staff will enter your room without permission. Your privacy will be respected at all times.'

There is a commitment also to safeguard a resident's place in the event of short-term admission to hospital and a promise that, if it is felt that a resident can cope no longer at the home, any future arrangements or plans will be discussed with the person as well as with relatives and doctor.

Underpinning this layer of the contract is a commitment from the staff to avoid, as far as is possible, the negative consequences of institutionalisation: their aim is that residents should retain a high level of responsibility for their own care. Alongside this is an equally firm commitment to go on caring for the resident well beyond the point at which a more traditional old people's home might have accepted the need for admission to a long-stay hospital bed.

The second layer of the contract is negotiated between each group of residents and the staff member responsible for their unit. As the brochure states: 'You will have a regular say in the everyday running of the home at the meetings between residents and staff.' Although there are occasional meetings where all residents and staff come together, the regular meetings take place in each unit: up to eight residents with one senior member of staff. The unit decides for itself how often to meet, who should act as chairperson and secretary, what should be discussed, and how decisions should be implemented. Issues which may be aired vary from basic problems of group living to the organisation of special events. Each unit develops its own unique agreement which changes and develops according to the needs and wishes of the group of residents. The meetings, and the decisions which result from them, provide one forum for the regular renegotiation around the main feature of the basic agreement: that in return for preserving the right of each resident to personal independence and choice, and personal responsibility for their actions, the home staff will expect residents to do as much as possible for themselves.

The third layer of the agreement involves the development of a care-plan for each resident. Residents are normally admitted, in the first instance, on a trial basis for six weeks. At this stage a review is held, to which the resident can invite anybody they wish. At this review, which is usually attended by the resident, their social worker and at least one relative or close friend, as well as by staff from the home, a decision is reached whether or not to offer a permanent place. Such an offer is hardly ever withheld, but a few residents do decide at this point that they could continue to manage at home, perhaps with increased community support.

During the first six weeks the resident's key worker will have been assessing how much responsibility for self-care it is reasonable to expect this resident to accept. After experiment, discussions and negotiation, a provisional care-plan is drawn up before the review, where it is either amended or endorsed. It will then be updated annually or after any significant change in the resident's state of health. The care-plan which follows was drawn up for an old lady of 79 who was nearly blind on admission, and had come to the home three years earlier from a large establishment run on traditional lines where she has resided for thirteen years. This is the fourth version of the original care-plan.

Name: Miss Violet O'Neill.
Date of birth: 4.6.02.
Date of admission: 9.1.81.
Date of original contract: 6.2.81.
Update one: 21.6.82.
Update two: 30.10.83.

Background.   Little known of early life. No immediate family. Lived with brother and sister-in-law until admitted to the Grange in 1968. Has only shared accommodation with women since. Was described as 'simple' and has apparently never been able to hold down a job. She had become institutionalised during her thirteen years at the Grange: residents and staff appear to have regarded her as somewhat of a nuisance. Therefore, she was deprived socially.

Family and outside contacts.   Her step-sister, also quite elderly and frail, is interested in Violet but cannot visit. She writes occasionally. She has a daughter who does visit occasionally and will try to come if Violet is ill or worried about anything.

Personality.   Violet is now well able to communicate her desires and wishes and can look after herself in the unit. Indeed, one or two residents are frightened of Violet's greater physical strength which, although never used, means that greater notice is sometimes taken of her wants. She is also quite strong and digs her heels in to get her way. Violet has a very moral outlook and is not easily swayed.

Health and mobility.   Violet's mobility is greatly impaired by her almost total blindness and increasing hearing difficulties, but she is learning to get around remarkaby well in the bungalow where she is familiar with the lay-out. Her breathlessness is the result of a chronic chest condition that needs occasional courses of antibiotics to help her through the worst time.

Social activities and interests. Is taken to church every Sunday by a volunteer driver (is a keen Methodist). Attends the Blind Club on the first Wednesday of each month. Taxi collects her at 1.30p.m. and she is back at about 5p.m. She enjoys Friday craft sessions and welcomes any opportunity to attend and join in any activities or outings.

Daily living activities and personal routine. Violet has become a very independent lady who has worked out her own routine and will ask when she needs assistance from staff.

    Pension. Division deals with pension. Has her own building society account.

    Dressing. Self. Needs help getting things out of her wardrobe where she keeps things in strict order and knows exactly where everything is. Also needs to be encouraged to change underwear daily.

    Breakfast. Enjoys a cooked breakfast. Betty (another resident) makes her tea, lays the table, and does her bread and butter. Usually has a poached egg: needs staff to cook this for her.

    Lunch. Staff need to serve lunch up for her and cut things up. Uses her own special plate and spoons which she finds less messy and easier to manage.

    Tea. Needs help as with lunch. Often would rather a sandwich made up for her. Is well able to tell you what she wants put in it.

    Washing-up. As rota. Sometimes needs help to make sure dishes are sorted into appropriate piles and that she has washing-up liquid put in the water. Because she is so willing, Violet often gets put upon by other residents, doing more than her fair share. Always washes as she has difficult seeing to wipe. Washes her own breakfast things.

    Personal laundry. Violet will ask for help when she wants her laundry done. She enjoys doing this herself and needs assistance to use the machine and dryer. Her ironing is done the next day. Violet needs careful supervision but is quite certain about wanting to take part.

    Bathing. Saturday evening and Wednesday morning. She needs help in and out of the bath and with hair-washing. Likes to have curlers put in her hair when it is washed.

    Bedmaking. Self. Minimum supervision needed. Changes sheets with help.

    Cleaning. Always keeps her own rooms very tidy. Cleaned by domestics once a week.

Individual programme objectives.
1. To maintain Violet's new-found independence while, at the same time, recognising her increasing blindness.
2. Making sure that she is not excluded from day-to-day activities and decisions within the home because of these communication difficulties.

This example of the third layer of the contract, the agreement drawn up between the resident and her key worker, illustrates how the general principle of offering a high level of personal independence and choice, in return for maximum responsibility for self-care on the part of each resident, has been worked out with one resident with special needs. The existence of such a care-plan does not eliminate the difficulties for all those concerned in ensuring that the principles are put into action, but it does provide a framework into which the transactions between residents and staff can be structured. If Violet suddenly decides not to do her personal laundry, her key worker has a basis on which to challenge this change in her behaviour. If a staff member forgets that Violet likes to have a bath on Saturday evening, Violet has the right to complain without being labelled 'difficult'. This structure does not neutralise the emotional dynamics which develop in any dependency relationship, but it does offer some scope for managing them constructively. Additionally, it offers a defence against the tendency in any institution for the residents to abandon and staff to take over all responsibility for decision-making and their personal care.

Issues in Groupwork.
Four issues arise in groupwork which pose certain problems for workers who wish to negotiate agreements.

Individual v. Group Needs.
This issue has been considered already in relation to residential work. The needs of each individual group member will be rather different. Some of them may be in conflict with other people's needs or with the needs of the group as a whole. For example, in a group of adolescent boys, one member may have been brought up in a very rigid family where any challenge to the existing order would provoke an authoritarian response. Other members may have been brought up in families where no appropriate limits were set and where they have had little experience of adults saying 'no' and meaning it. It may prove difficult to negotiate an agreement about reasonable limits of behaviour and how workers should respond, in a way which meets the needs of all members, when they are breached.

Another aspect of this issue is whether contracts are required with individual group members in addition to with the group as a whole. The answer depends on the objectives of the group. Where these are group-centred, that is, where the main emphasis is on what the group as a whole can achieve, for example in social groups and social action groups, an agreement is needed with the group. Where the objectives are individual–centred, that is, where the main emphasis is on individual change, agreements will be needed with each group member in addition to a contract with the whole group.

Who Identifies the Need?
In most forms of social work a need has been expressed by the time the

social worker and client meet. Whether or not the need has been expressed by people other than the client, the client will usually be aware of the issue which has led to the contact. Groupwork differs in that the initiative to offer help and to bring people together is usually taken by the workers. Consequently, members may come to the first meeting with quite different ideas about what they want to obtain from the experience and about the potential usefulness of the group. There are likely to be quite wide divergencies in the aims of individual members. Where this is the case, where members do not initially accept the worker's definition of need or perceive that they have needs in common, in the first instance only a preliminary agreement may be possible. There may also be a power struggle between members, or between the members collectively and the workers, as to which needs should take priority. This area of conflict is not unique to groupwork, nor is it necessarily negative in its consequences, but it is more likely to arise openly in the contracting phase of groupwork than in other contexts.

Attachments to Other Systems

Another distinguishing feature of groupwork is that the participants are usually attached to and more heavily involved with other systems, for example their family, peer-groups and neighbours. Their entry into the system formed by the group creates a new situation but it will be unusual for the members to experience membership of the group as the strongest influence in their lives. This has two major consequences. First, the members will import into the group at least some aspects of the values of the systems whose culture they have already adopted and, insofar as members come from different backgrounds, there is likely to be tension and conflict when it comes to negotiating aims, objectives and rules. Secondly, the commitment which members are able to make to the contract which is agreed may come under pressure from the competing demands of family or peer-group.

Where possible, group workers need to anticipate the possible reactions of these significant other people to the aims of the group and to consider whether they can neutralise or overcome them. Otherwise, these people may feel threatened by, anxious or resentful of the member's use of the group and attempt to sabotage membership. For example, it may be helpful for group workers to explain to parents or partners the objectives of and minimum requirements for the group prior to negotiating a secondary agreement with them around the issues of enabling the member to attend and respecting the confidentiality of the group.

The Power of Group Dynamics.

Most groups, formed from a social worker's initiative, consist of people who do not have regular or frequent interaction outside the group.

Whereas families or residential communities spend most of their time together and enjoy long-standing relationships, groups brought together by social workers have to establish norms and rules, determine who should adopt leadership and other roles, develop a group identity and cope with emerging likes and dislikes between members in addition to tackling the work of the group. Groups, therefore, pass through a series of characteristic stages in their life. (Preston-Shoot,1987).

These dynamics inevitably affect the process of negotiating contracts. Individuals making leadership bids may contribute to the contracting process for reasons which are as much to do with their attempt to achieve leadership as to do with their views on the content of the contract. Equally, the group may go through a phase in which members need to externalise the problem. If the contract is negotiated when the group is in that phase of its life, it may need to be renegotiated when that phase has been passed. Workers often begin by being very central to the group's development and work. However, as the group establishes its norms, defines its tasks and embarks on its programme, the group workers may seek to encourage the members to assume greater responsibility for the maintenance, direction and work of the group. Awareness of these processes, which may affect the negotiation of a contract, does not protect the worker from being caught up in them at the time but may be valuable at the planning stage and in conducting analyses of the session after the group. Awareness of these processes may lead group workers to negotiate different agreements as their groups pass through the stages of joining, beginning the work, revision, renewed emphasis on the work and termination. Alternatively, as the stages are not unidirectional or sequential, group workers may negotiate one agreement with the group at the outset which anticipates the stages that groups can pass through and builds in that flexibility.

Example 5:3. A Contract with a Group of Parents Whose Children are 'Beyond Control'

This example is taken from a 'pilot' group, organised and run as an experiment to test whether it was the kind of group which clients would find useful. The idea was based on the belief that parents with a child who is regarded as 'beyond parental control' feel isolated in their neigbourhood because neighbours are often the victims of the child's unacceptable behaviour. They also feel guilty because parents are generally seen as blameworthy when young children appear to be out of control. The agreement was negotiated in the first two sessions.

1. The group will meet for seven sessions on Tuesdays: 9.30–11 a.m.
2. The group workers will provide transport to and from the group. A crêche will be provided for young children.
3. The group workers will record the content of each group discussion

and provide each member with copies of their notes.
4. The group will use two meetings to discuss each of these areas:
   a) what social workers can do to help parents who feel that their children are beyond control.
   b) what community changes would help parents.
   c) what family changes would help parents.
5. The group workers will arrange for police officers to attend one group meeting to discuss community policing.
6. A meeting will be arranged, in addition to the group, so that group members can discuss their concerns as parents with local social workers and can explore how parents can participate more actively in decisions made on what services social workers offer.
7. The group will discuss what changes members want/need and possibly invite other people in positions of power to the group for discussions.
8. The final meeting of the group will be a review to discuss what might follow on from this pilot group.

Comment   This contract is an interim agreement, more reciprocal than mutual. Since it was a pilot group and the workers were uncertain whether there was either a demand for it or whether it would be of value to the participants, there was a limited timescale. The workers had other objectives which they did not share with the members at this stage: they wanted the group to provide a forum for reflective discussion which might help the members to recognise their own contribution to the maintenance of the problem in a non-blameworthy way. They hoped also that the experience of group membership might help the parents to develop more confidence and to become more assertive with their children, by supporting each other in this process. In the initial exploratory discussions it was clear that the parents were highly resistant to the ideas upon which the workers' objectives were based. They saw the problems as based in the community in which they lived .d exacerbated by the weak responses of the police and social services. The agreement was, therefore, both an interim one in that the workers had longer-term objectives which they felt might be more acceptable if introduced later, and reciprocal rather than mutual in that the demands for input from the police and local social workers came from the parents and were not seen as intrinsically useful by the social workers, whereas the demand in clause 4c to discuss what family changes might help the parents was made by the workers and did not appear to be seen as valuable by the parents.

With hindsight, it is easy to recognise that part of the pressure to externalise the problem and blame the lack of community resources was the result of the dynamics involved in the early stages of the group. It was safer for members to identify and focus on an external common enemy than to expose their own weaknesses in the group. A group, run over a longer period, would have benefited from a preliminary contract.

This would allow the issues to be explored over several sessions, leaving the main contract to be negotiated after the dynamics involved in the process of forming a new group had been worked through.

Example 5:4 Contracts with the Parties Involved in an Intermediate Treatment Group

This example is taken from a group for adolescent boys who were becoming involved in delinquent activities. Although the group was funded as part of the Intermediate Treatment programme, attendance was not compulsory as part of a Supervision Order imposed by the juvenile court. The agreements involved contracts with each boy, his parents, the referring social worker and the group as a whole. Negotiations took place during the phase in which the boys were offered membership of the group and in the first two meetings of the group. The agreements cover framework issues: the basic rules and expectations, for example in relation to attendance; and issues of substance: the aim of the group, what the workers are offering and what members are committing themselves to.

a) Contract with Tim
1. Tim agrees to attend the group and to be on time. If he cannot attend, he will make sure that the group workers are informed.
2. Tim agrees not to threaten or abuse the workers and other members. He will not leave the group before the end of each session and will behave in a reasonable manner.
3. Tim agrees to join in the activities and group discussions.
4. Tim agrees not to commit further offences.
5. The group workers want Tim to attend the group and will organise a programme for the group. If Tim has suggestions about the programme, the workers will try to include these.
6. The group workers will organise and attend review meetings which will monitor Tim's progress in the group. They will keep everyone informed of Tim's progress, behaviour and attendance.

b) Contract with Tim's parents
1. Mr and Mrs Cotton agree to Tim attending the group and have been told by the groupworkers what will be expected of Tim in the group.
2. They agree to encourage Tim to attend the group and fulfil his agreement with the group workers.
3. They agree to attend review meetings and to discuss Tim's progress with the group workers.

c) Contract with Eric, the referring social worker
1. Eric wants Tim to attend the group and understands what the group involves.
2. Eric has provided some information about Tim and his family, has discussed this with the family and will keep the groupworkers informed of any significant developments.
3. Eric will maintain regular contact with Tim and the group workers

during the duration of the group. He will attend review meetings and complete the evaluation questionnaire at the end of the group.

d) Contract with the group

1. The group will meet on Wednesday between 5 and 7 p.m.
2. Members of the group will make their own way to the group. Their fares will be reimbursed. Group members will be taken home.
3. The group will meet for twenty sessions and end with a residential weekend.
4. Members agree to join in all the activities planned by the group workers. Each meeting will begin with a discussion about future activities and members will be able to make suggestions.
5. Review meetings will be held with the group after ten sessions and at the end of the group. If anyone wants to discuss the group at other times, they may request a meeting.
6. The group has agreed to the following rules:
   a)   no smoking or fighting.
   b)   to leave the group sessions only with permission.
   c)   to inform the workers if they are unable to attend.
7. Any reports written by the group workers will be discussed with the group.
8. The group has been organised in the hope of helping members not to commit further offences. Accordingly, the group workers have organised the following activities:
   a)   a meeting with community constables and juvenile bureau officers.
   b)   visits to local community centres and youth clubs.
   c)   discussions and role-plays about offending.
   d)   opportunities to develop members' interests, for example learning how to swim.
9. If members do not attend regularly, a review meeting will be held with the member, his parents and social worker.
10. If the group's rules are broken, the group will hold its own review meeting.

Comment   The contracts with Tim's parents and the referring social worker were secondary agreements, whereas the contracts with Tim and the group were primary agreements. They were also mainstream agreements because the workers had substantial information about the boys who had been referred and had given detailed information to local social workers about the type of group they intended to run when seeking referrals. The position of these agreements on the mutual–reciprocal dimension depends on one's judgement about how strongly each boy wanted to keep out of further trouble and what cost to their personal freedom they were prepared to pay to achieve that objective. The contract with Tim includes considerations which are sufficient (clauses 1–3) and a consideration which is insufficient (clause 4) because of the criminal and civil law. The contracts could be extended to incorporate what we have labelled as substance. For instance, the contract with Tim could include clauses on the problems or difficulties for which he is requesting help. Similar clauses could be written into the agreements with the social worker and Tim's parents, noting the difficulties which they believe Tim is experiencing or objectives and priorities which they believe to be important.

Conclusion

This chapter has considered some of the special features of both residential work and groupwork and the way they are liable to affect the process of negotiating contracts. We have given examples of some contrasting use of the concept in both contexts. Much more detailed work needs to be done in adapting the broad principles of this working concept to the specific contexts in which social workers find themselves employed. In this chapter we have taken some tentative steps in this direction in two specific areas but more sophisticated analyses need to be undertaken by specialists in the relevant areas of practice.

6   A Step-by-Step Practice Model

Introduction
This chapter will discuss the stages in the process of negotiating, implementing and reviewing a contract and will present a step-by-step model for using contracts in any social work intervention. Dividing the process into separate stages may appear artificial when in the real world each step merges into and overlaps with the next. However, elaborating each stage separately may enable practitioners to identify, develop and use core practice skills in social work intervention within a contractual approach and to adopt a structured, systematic and evaluative approach to their practice.

A Step-by-Step Model
Figure 6.1 outlines the different stages of using contracts in social work. Each stage requires the application of one or more of the core skills of social work. At the end of each stage a key question is posed, one which requires an affirmative answer if the parties are to proceed to the next stage.

Step 1: Initial Contact
Here the social worker's main priority is to listen to those who have the problem or who are seeking change. Listening may include asking the questions which enable the clients to describe what they need. Practitioners must accept responsibility also for creating a climate in which those in need of help can talk freely. The importance of the client–worker relationship is well established. Successful process and outcome do seem related to the extent to which practitioners can instil hope, create a warm and accepting relationship seen by clients as potentially helpful and communicate that change is possible. At an emotional level the worker has to establish a basis of understanding: if the client senses that a degree of empathy exists and feels supported and understood, the subsequent processes of negotiation are more likely to succeed.

The other responsibility resting on social workers at this stage is to make clear to clients how the function of their agency connects with the clients' problems. The potential client may be very unsure what services or help they can expect from an agency or they may be very clear what is needed and where to get it. Social workers need to establish the position of each client in this respect and to explain whether and in what way the agency might respond to their particular issues.

Initial contacts should offer potential clients an accurate representation of how they are likely to be treated if agreement is reached to embark on further work. The personal qualities of genuineness, warmth and the ability to develop and sustain an appropriate level of empathy need to be visible (Truax and Carkhuff, 1967). To be effective all parties must see that they will get something out of the process. Clients need to feel valued, accepted and engaged before they can be expected to see the benefits or rationale behind what is being offered. To deliver on what one promises and not to commit the agency or oneself beyond what one can deliver are also particularly important at this stage.

The key question is to establish whether the problem or need which is presented is one which the agency can meet and, if it is not, whether it conceals another problem which is appropriate for the agency. If these questions cannot be answered affirmatively there is no basis for moving on to subsequent stages in the process of negotiating a contract. If the problem is concealed or camouflaged the worker needs to test whether it can be brought out into the open. The negotiations with the Jackson family, described in Chapter 3, illustrate this process. The health visitor had referred this case originally to the Social Services Department, which decided that the deprivation caused by the long-standing disconnection of electricity was not a problem for which their agency could or should offer a service. They advised the health visitor to refer the family to the Family Service Unit. Our agency's response might have been the same on the grounds that we could not offer effective help to all families whose electricity supply was disconnected. However, our observations suggested both that the parents had exhausted all other sources of help with this problem and that their inability to solve it was placing an intolerable strain on the health and morale of some family members.

Step 2: Planning
Social workers are expected to be helpful and to provide solutions. Frequently too they encounter a high level of distrust from potential clients. These two pressures can create a sense of obligation to produce the instant answer or, at the other extreme, conscious of the scarcity of resources, to emphasise a gate-keeping and/or authority role and a crisis-oriented, business-like approach at the expense of promoting individual welfare and conveying warmth, genuineness and empathy. Either of these reactions may be both the result of and a contributing factor to a lack of planning. Before social workers can answer the questions of what help consumers need or what needs to change, a clear picture of the situation is required, a focus on identifying and elaborating the problem. Insufficient planning may result in practitioners misconstruing the task, misreading the help that is being requested and/or feeling muddled and uncertain.

Figure 6.1   Step-by-step model

Step	Negotiating task	Emotional task
1. Initial contact	Listening to the client. Explaining agency function	Engagement. Establishing empathy.
2. Planning.	Collecting information: assessment. Initial definition of the problem. Identifying methods/resources to achieve change.	Detachment/ objectivity without losing empathy.
3. Identifying potential action-systems.	Exploring with relevant others the extent of their willingness to join in the change process. Clarifying agency's commitment to bring about change.	Generating hope and optimism
4 Identifying an acceptable/appropriate contract.	Clarifying the extent/ limit of the client's willingness to begin work.	Offering partnership. Holding onto own/agency position without rejecting the client.
5. Drawing up the terms of the contract and defining targets.	Specifying aims, objectives and methods to be used. Specifying the degree of agreement. Identifying target-systems.	Enabling clients' views and position to be respected.
6. Securing agreement.	Establishing intention and commitment of the parties involved. Taking account of fears/ anxieties. Specifying obligations.	Exchange: give and take. Promises for services.
7. Implementing the agreement.	Keeping to the task while avoiding inflexibility. Performing roles. Analysis/ recording.	Support and encouragement. Listening for doubts or changes in circumstances.
8. Review.	Does the problem still exist? Improvement or deterioration (outcome)? In spite of or because of the work (process)? Is further work required? Is further work wanted?	Non-judgemental attitude. Willingness to accept criticism. Standing back from precision of contract to look at overall change.

Legal Term	Process
Invitation to treat.	Is the need one which the agency should meet? Yes.　　　No ⟶ Explain. Refer on if appropriate
	Is the problem capable of resolution or alleviation? Yes.　　　No ⟶ Will this involve agency in some other way? Care proceedings or after criminal trial? Client may need less structured support. Can this be offered?
	Are resources likely to be made available? Yes.　　　No ⟶ Why not? Does this need advocacy/pressure through appropriate channels?
Offer, acceptance and communication of acceptance Intention to contract.	Is there a basic willingness to participate? Yes.　　　No ⟶ What are the obstacles? Is there serious mistrust? Can the problem be addressed in some other way (return to step two)?
Defects in contracts: duress, undue influenced incapacity.	Can an appropriate contract be drafted? Yes.　　　No ⟶ Analyse why not. Return to an earlier stage if appropriate.
Consideration.	Can agreement be obtained? Yes.　　　No ⟶ Either return to step five and select a different type of contract or return to step two.
	Is the agreement implemented? Yes.　　　No ⟶ Analyse why not. Return to step two or close.
Ending contracts: frustrated/rescission/ dispute/abandonment review/termination.	Has the work been successful in eliminating the problem resulting in further work not being necessary? Yes.　　　No ⟶ Analyse why not. This may involve a return to any of the preceding steps. Closure.

The planning stage, for which a preliminary contract may be negotiated, involves three main questions. First, what is known already about the situation? This question allows practitioners to formulate initial concerns or purposes and to anticipate the fears, uncertainties, concerns, attitudes and possible reactions of the client-system and target-systems. In the work with the Jackson family, Mr Jackson had preserved the correspondence between himself, the electricity board and the citizen's advice bureau over the previous three years. This proved extremely valuable in enabling an assessment of the likely negotiating stance of the Electricity Board. In the case of Miss O'Neill's agreement with the staff of the old people's home, there was considerable information about what she could and could not do, and how far she was affected by her increasing blindness. This enabled the staff and Miss O'Neill to reach agreement about the revised 'care-plan' relatively easily. In other situations the information may be negative. For example, a social worker might identify the need to provide a group for young boys on the fringes of delinquent behaviour by discovering the absence of any suitable facilities on a particular estate.

This existing information can be supplemented and modified by enabling the participants to define the problems, for example through the following sequence of questions: what is the problem? who is it a problem for? why is it a problem and why now? why is help being sought and why now? what solutions have been tried and with what effect? In answering the questions 'why' and 'what' the requirement is for specificity, for dividing each problem into smaller, more manageable and less overwhelming parts.

The second question is whether, on the basis of initial contacts and of the information already available, the worker can generate any coherent explanation of the origin and maintenance of the identified problem. There is considerable debate within social work about whether practitioners need to understand the causes and history of a problem to intervene successfully, and whether social problems can and should be analysed and resolved on the basis of a linear and unicausal model rather than on a model based on the systems concepts of equifinality and circularity.[1] However, in any situation workers need to be clear at least how much of a working hypothesis is needed before an agreement can be negotiated to cover the process of intervention. In Miss O'Neill's case, the explanation of her difficulties in maintaining her independence was clearly adequate for the needs of the workers. With the Jacksons it was useful to understand how the debt arose, if only to anticipate what help might be needed to avoid a repetition, but this understanding would not have been essential to achieve the primary objective.

The third question requires practitioners to identify their own fears about entering into agreements. Using contracts implies a level of commitment which social workers may experience as quite threatening. Whether or not they are experienced and have firmly identified their skills and resources, it is not uncommon for practitioners to be apprehensive, to lack confidence and to doubt whether they can live up to the commitment required by contracts. These anxieties may find expression in fears or fantasies concerned with losing control of the negotiations, facing unreasonable demands, meeting obstructive resistance or encountering suspicion which prevents the participants from engaging in a collaborative endeavour. Even if these fears rarely materialise in practice they can influence the worker's initial approach to the task of planning for a viable contract. It is important to be able to share them in supervision and for workers to clarify how much time they can commit themselves to if a regular programme of work is being considered. Unless workers receive some protection from the demands of every crisis or emergency they will be unable to honour the commitment to meet regularly with and provide specific services for their clients. Equally, to present to clients the opportunities which this method of working offers, to communicate the purpose behind using contracts, and to instil motivation and confidence in consumers who may be uncertain about or unfamiliar with this method of work, practitioners themselves must feel comfortable with it.

The key question which must be answered affirmatively for the process to move on to the next stage is whether the identified problem is one which is capable of resolution or alleviation as a result of social work intervention. Some problems clearly fall outside the scope of social workers. For example, parents may find it impossible to meet their family's basic needs on supplementary benefit even when all additional entitlements have been obtained. When welfare rights advocacy cannot obtain additional benefits and when the family cannot economise more frugally, there may be no other help the social worker can offer. In another situation, parents may be failing very evidently to meet a child's basic needs but may deny that a problem exists. This may rule out the possibility of any work based on a contract although it will almost certainly involve the agency in some other role, using its statutory powers to remove and protect the child. Contracts work best when potential solutions to problems lie substantially within the gift of those directly involved, when each party genuinely possesses the power to alter things for the others (Sheldon, 1980), when clients are able to act to alleviate the problems with the worker as an agent in the task, and when the problems fall within the scope of their combined resources (Reid and Epstein, 1972).

In this second stage the worker may need to step back to make a more detached and objective assessment of the client's situation without losing the basis of understanding and empathy already established. Here again, the supervisor's role can be crucial in helping the worker to achieve that difficult balance.

Step 3: Identifying Potential Action-Systems

Having identified a problem with the client which is capable, in principle, of responding to social work intervention, the next task is to gather information from significant others: professionals and neighbours or relatives engaged in supporting somebody in the community. Except in emergencies or situations where it has been impossible to establish even the minimum level of understanding with the client, the process of gathering information should be with the client's permission. It continues to be a source of concern how freely agencies expect to be able to share highly confidential information about the users of their services.

The process of collecting information can be combined often with a process of exploring whether and how far the parties who have some significant involvement in the client's life are prepared to contribute their influence or resources to attack the problem. This lays the foundation for negotiating secondary contracts without which the primary agreement between worker and client may be rendered ineffectual.

Often the potential action-system, those with whom practitioners need to deal and secure secondary agreements in order to accomplish tasks and achieve the identified objectives, will be familiar already to the worker. In these circumstances this stage may be completed rapidly, almost routinely, but there are dangers here. First, although the worker may be familiar with the route, the client may be in unexplored territory and the practitioner may neglect to share their knowledge. Secondly, the worker may select prematurely a course of action with which they are familiar because to routinise problems makes work more manageable. This may result in the worker leading the client in a direction they do not wish to travel.

The importance and value of establishing the attitude of significant others before a firm contract is established cannot be over-emphasised. Contracts can be frustrated by the indifference, hostility, different objectives or incomprehension of members within the client's informal networks or representatives of societal welfare agencies. This dimension dominates much social work practice and provides many opportunities but also some constraints for negotiating deals on behalf of clients (Whittington, 1983).

In this stage workers will often find that they are confronted by pessimism or disillusionment. Most problems only reach them when relatives, neighbours and other societal agencies have offered advice or solutions already which have been tried in vain or rejected. A central task, therefore, will often be to generate hope and optimism. The power of hope as an ingredient of positive change has long been recognised (Smale, 1977) but the role of social workers in rekindling the embers of optimism at the start of a change-effort, when a potential action-system is being formulated, has not always been acknowledged.

The key question here is whether sufficient resources will be made available to achieve the changes required. Whether these resources consist of the worker's time, energy and use of self or of day nursery places, domiciliary physiotherapy or short-stay residential care, practitioners cannot move onto the next stage until they feel assured that they have the means to address the problem, that they can provide the services which the client wants or which are appropriate to the needs defined.

Step 4: Identifying an Appropriate and Acceptable Contract

With assessment having been a continuous process in each of the stages outlined already, this is the point where workers have to decide the kind of help they can offer. Specific treatment models may be considered, such as task-centred casework, behaviour modification, systemic family therapy or groupwork. Alternatively, the help may comprise mobilising and coordinating a package of resources from various sources to meet the multiplicity of needs identified. Sometimes the offer may be more restrictive, a statement about how a worker intends to exercise the statutory authority vested in their agency.

To some extent this process may be identified in any client–worker transaction. What is unique to this model is that the criteria for proposing a particular approach include active testing-out of the acceptability of that approach for the client. Some problems are obviously more likely to respond to behaviour modification than to family therapy. Some workers know more about task-centred casework than about non-directive counselling. Both these factors should be taken into account. However, whereas these two factors, especially the second, are already influential in determining the form in which help is offered, the 'contract' model gives equal weight to a third factor: in what form is the help most likely to be acceptable to the client? It is *not* argued that this should be the determining factor. It *is* proposed that it should be weighed in the balance.

It is beyond the scope of this book to discuss indicators for and against particular methods of work. However, another question which must be answered is how workers decide who is the client. For staff of an old people's home, for instance, it may seem obvious that the residents are the clients. However, when a confused and frail old person is newly admitted and the staff propose a 'care-plan' in which the resident is expected to take some responsibility for his/her own daily care, what is the status of a relative's objection that the resident has not taken responsibility for doing the washing-up or personal laundry for the last five years? The admission may have been arranged more for the relative's benefit and it probably would have been the relative who requested help in the first instance. Perhaps the relative is the client rather than the new resident in which case our model would appear to imply that the help should be offered in a form which is acceptable to the relative.

This problem has no simple solution. However, two guidelines can be helpful in deciding at any point who is the client. The first is a recognition that, as each social situation changes, so will the assigned roles of the parties. Therefore, in the example outlined above, although it may have been necessary and appropriate to regard the relative as the client or, at least, as part of the client-system up to the point of admission, the event of admission creates a new and quite different situation. The second guideline draws on social work's value-base which is legitimately located in concern for the disadvantaged and oppressed. Social workers have an obligation in any situation to attempt to ensure that the needs of the disadvantaged or oppressed are attended to. When a probation officer is asked to prepare a social enquiry report, the client initially may be the court which is seeking guidance on the appropriate sentence. However, the probation officer has an obligation, usually acknowledged and welcomed by the court, to explore the offender's social situation in order to ascertain whether they are sufficiently disadvantaged to justify the court in setting aside its punitive role and instead offering a helping relationship in which the offender and/or the family become the client.

The crucial task here, then, is to establish the extent of any common ground between the agency and the client-system. Can effective help be offered in a form which will be acceptable to the client? This assumes that clients and practitioners are engaged and have established a relationship. However, it is prudent not to take this for granted because a variety of factors may inhibit clients from talking openly. They may have found previous encounters with professionals dissatisfying or may experience a sense of stigma and failure in asking for help. They may be afraid that social work intervention will expose personal weaknesses or bring to the interaction stereotypes about social workers, for example that they take children away. They may be fearful about what will happen if they participate or anxious about their ability to engage with the worker. As part of demonstrating an active and positive understanding and of being open and receptive to the client's position, practitioners should explore any feelings clients may hold about receiving assistance. They may find it appropriate to name the client's fear of what might happen or to acknowledge it as legitimate or to challenge the client's view, for example that seeking help is a sign of weakness. They should avoid vague statements such as wanting to help because these can create resistance since clients will be uncertain about the worker's intentions or perception of the situation. Social workers should provide an explanation as to why contracts are beneficial to workers and clients alike. They should make clear their intentions at the outset and point out that the process of understanding the situation and negotiating a contract may take several sessions to complete. As part of this process, it may be helpful to prepare a summary of each meeting to be shared with clients at the beginning of the next session to ensure agreement on what has been discussed and to pick up the threads of the negotiations. Finally, social workers should distinguish an invitation to treat from an offer of services since clients might assume otherwise that they are required to use all the services a practitioner can offer.

The key question before moving on to the next stage is whether there is a basic willingness to participate in the effort which is being proposed. If the answer is yes, practitioners can proceed to specifying the aims and drawing up the terms of the agreement. A negative answer may send them back to stage 2, to considering if the problem or need is one which can be resolved or alleviated.

Step 5: Specifying Aims and Objectives and Drawing up the Terms of the Agreement

Chapter 4 outlined what should be covered in an agreement. Clearly the complexity of any agreement will depend considerably on the extent of an agency's responsibility for the problem and the likely course of events. An agreement covering the process of helping a disabled person secure any necessary aids and adaptations may not need to be so complex as an agreement covering that person's admission into long-term residential care. Nor do all agreements need to take the form of written documents since in some situations the existence of or need to draw up a written document may impede the speed or flexibility of the response. However, we would recommend that, even where it is not considered appropriate to draw up a formal written agreement, workers keep full notes outlining what they consider to be the contract's essential features.

The crucial task in this stage is to ensure that agreements cover the areas which are essential as a minimum basis for starting work together. In drawing up the terms, workers need to ensure that clients' views and anxieties are properly represented. In cases where clients may be regarded as incapable of entering into agreements or as having accepted offers under some form of duress, particular care must be taken to ensure that their position is not misrepresented. Some possible safeguards were proposed in Chapter 3. More generally, practitioners must ensure that clients do not sense their participation to be compulsory. For contracts to be effective, not only must clients feel their agreements to be appropriate and relevant but also the power imbalance between clients and workers must be acknowledged. Otherwise agreements may be based on social workers' wishes internalised by clients as 'shoulds and oughts'. Put another way, whilst social workers may encourage consumers to state their objectives, clients may place considerable weight on either what they see as or what practitioners express as their targets for change. In these situations practitioners can easily abuse the worker–client relationship and, unwittingly, reduce the space clients have to articulate their aims and wishes. The task is to ensure that clients have been able to say what they want, based on an understanding of the available alternatives.

Before moving on, the key question of whether an appropriate contract can be drafted has three sub-questions. First, is there a basis of agreement on key issues? As explained in Chapter 4 mutual agreement is not essential but participants should not commit themselves to a contract unless they feel able to enter fully into the bargain. Where agreements are more reciprocal than mutual each party must accept that it has the cooperation of the other and be willing to assist in achieving that party's objectives in order to achieve its own goals. Whilst it is not necessary to share a common purpose or goal, contracts are more effective where the balance of agreement or acceptable aims is stronger than the areas of disagreement, and where it is possible to work within and respect different goals. It is better to agree substantially on something small than partially and with difficulty on something grand since it is better to be realistic and to enable agreements to prove their worth in the short-term in order for them to have a chance to prove themselves in the long term (Sheldon, 1980).

Secondly, are the client's fears, anxieties and resistance adequately acknowledged and catered for? Have practitioners been able to elicit and explore any doubts or misgivings which clients may harbour about the intervention? The task of dealing with the problems with which they are concerned may be frustrated if practitioners and clients are unable to talk openly.

Thirdly, can the aims, objectives and methods be articulated clearly? The clearer these are, the more able clients will be to accept offers of services and to make alternative or supplementary suggestions; and the less likely practitioners will be to commit themselves to objectives they cannot achieve or to a process which drifts into the longer term. Terms must be specific since vague language may be interpreted differently by those involved. Objectives, defined in terms of changes the parties would ideally like and be satisfied with, and tasks should be manageable and realistic. Time-limits should be feasible, sufficient for the work to be undertaken. If the goals and changes are reasonable, if there is agreement on what needs to change, on what change is needed and on how to attempt change, a cooperative client–worker relationship is more likely to develop. The wider the goals and changes desired, the more likely contracts are to fail (Sheldon, 1980).

If these questions can be answered affirmatively practitioners can proceed. If drafting an agreement proves difficult or impossible it indicates the need to return to an earlier stage or, if necessary, to abandon negotiations altogether.

Step 6: Securing Agreement

Often a special meeting may be needed to go through the specific terms of the contract, amend any proposals which are not entirely acceptable and invite the various parties formally to endorse the agreement. Where such formality is inappropriate, the fact that an agreement has been reached still needs to be acknowledged.

When agreement is reached it is crucial that every effort be made to ensure that all parties understand what they are agreeing to and what might happen if the agreement is breached or if the parties find it unacceptable in practice (for example, review; invoking statutory powers; rescission where unrestricted by statute). Any lack of enthusiasm or doubts should be taken seriously. To assume consensus or to push clients towards it is to court failure and disillusionment. Establishing intention to contract is difficult. Many clients have been 'social worked to death' in the past by agencies which have become involved and then withdrawn without any clear explanation. Why should they take seriously the demands of a new, uncomfortable intruder to make commitments which require forethought, trust and change (Preston-Shoot *et al.,* 1984)? Clients may be used to relying on social workers as experts with knowledge and solutions. They may be over-eager to agree or say what they believe is expected in order to fulfil roles they anticipate are expected of them. Past encounters with professionals or the experience of powerlessness, isolation and helplessness may lead them to doubt the value and scope of participation, the commitments they make and the consideration they have to exchange. Practitioners need to demonstrate honesty and openness with a clear belief that this approach can alter the situation significantly. Any pseudo-agreement, whether to please or to obtain services, must be challenged. The potential for cooperation and commitment should exist. When clients do not acknowledge a problem nor express a willingness to play an active role in overcoming it and to honour the terms of an agreement, contracts are a waste of time (Sheldon, 1980).

Equally important to take seriously is the difficulty an agency may have in entering into an agreement which reflects the client's needs or wishes, either because of understandings it has already with other systems (for example, courts and fuel boards) or because its statutory duties and obligations prevent it from taking certain steps (for example, automatically revoking a care order on successful completion of objectives within a contract) or because the resources needed are in scarce supply and not directly under the control of the worker drawing up the agreement. Workers must be clear what agreements they can enter into.

If the parties do commit themselves to a contract confident that commitments will be honoured, they can move on. If no agreement can be reached, a more limited agreement may be needed for those areas where there are not irreconcilable differences of opinion (step 5) or the process may have to be abandoned.

Step 7: Implementing the Agreement

Since each piece of work is unique it is possible only to flag important areas here for workers concerning the continued relevance of the contract to the work as it proceeds. One danger is that workers especially will pay too much attention to delivering their side of the bargain. They must not neglect how clients experience them or the relationship which develops. Space may need to be created to allow clients to reflect on how they experience the worker's involvement and to tell them how they interpret their actions. The existence of a contract in no way diminishes the obligation on workers to check that the relationships they develop and maintain with clients remain serviceable.

A second concern to be monitored centres on the feelings aroused by the work which has been agreed in the contract. It may not always be possible to anticipate the nature or strength of feelings aroused by the work. The pace of the work may need to be slowed down to enable the parties to work through these feelings.

A third danger is that once the agreement has been drawn up and endorsed the work begins and the contract is forgotten. In other words the process becomes ritualised but once the ritual has been completed the agreement is no longer used to provide the structure for work. Client and practitioner collude to deny its existence in order to avoid the stress and pain of tackling their work together.

The crucial skill in this phase is to find the most effective balance between keeping to the task and responding to the feelings aroused by the work. Workers need to support and encourage clients in addressing the issues, to maintain a safe environment in which clients can attempt the work and, if necessary, risk failure. At the same time they have to be alert to cues indicating doubt or uncertainty or to changes in circumstances which may frustrate the original agreement. The key question to be answered as this stage draws to a close is whether the agreement has been implemented. Whatever the answer, the next and final stage is crucial.

Stage 8: Reviewing the Contract and the Work

Contracts and the situations they address are developing phenomena. Consensus and disagreements between parties will change over time. The reality may prove different from the expectation. Expectations concerning the worker's role may diverge, perhaps with clients expecting the worker to be an expert and more central to the change process than the practitioner wishes to be. Reviews, therefore, are an important part of a contract model of work. The review machinery provides an opportunity for any party to the agreement to voice dissatisfaction or to demand changes in the contract. It provides also a means of renegotiating agreements where changes in circumstances require this.

Where the parties have completed successfully the work they agreed to do together the review can be used to acknowledge and consolidate the positive changes which have taken place and then to terminate contact or to negotiate another agreement around other objectives already defined or fresh concerns which have arisen. Where agreements are failing it provides an opportunity to examine whether this is related to ends (objectives not agreed), to means (methods of reaching the objectives) or to process (inadequate or cross-communication, or no rules to change the rules and the structure of an outdated agreement). Given any one of these scenarios, the initial contract will have become irrelevant to the current situation. The review process allows for revision or ending.

Obviously a balance is needed between holding reviews so often that the contract is always being changed and holding them so infrequently that only the most imprecise agreement could cover all the changes that take place. Fixing a review date when the agreement is negotiated can help the parties to maintain a clear focus. In our experience, a series of relevant, if short-lived agreements is more often effective than a portmanteau agreement which covers every eventuality over a long period.

Meetings to review agreements might follow the structure set out below: all parties to the agreement would be invited to attend.

1. The chairperson will explain the purpose of the meeting and refer to the original agreement and to the aims spelled out there.
2. The worker primarily responsible for the direct work or for co-ordinating a package of resources will have prepared a written summary of the work done which will have been circulated normally to all those present in advance of the meeting. The chairperson will ask whether the summary presents a fair and accurate picture.
3. Any areas of disagreement are noted and discussed.
4. Any other members of the action-system present at the review will be invited to add their comments. If they are not present their views should have been sought prior to the meeting.
5. The clients will be invited to give their views of the work: what they have found helpful; what they have found difficult, painful or unhelpful; what has been achieved.
6. This should lead on to a discussion about the present situation: is it acceptable or does more work need to be done? Have there been new developments which require attention? If the original problems have been resolved, has this created space and energy to tackle other important issues?
7. If further work is needed, should the original contract be revised or does it need a totally new agreement?
8. If no further work is needed, can the parties agree to end the work at once or is a 'disengagement' contract needed?

Clearly, the review exercise demands of the worker skills of detachment and objectivity mentioned in the planning stage: has the client's situation improved or deteriorated? Are the changes attributable to the work or to extraneous events? What has facilitated or impeded the process of intervention? A non-condemnatory attitude also needs to be conveyed. If the work has failed it is unhelpful if the clients feel they are to blame for the failure. It needs to be clear also that the worker can accept criticism or the client often will feel inhibited from speaking openly.

The key question here is whether the need and the motivation exist for further work. If the answer is yes, the next step may involve a return to stages 2, 3 or 4: to considering revised or new target areas and objectives, the resources needed and available, and what is/is not negotiable for each party. If the answer is no, the point has probably come when client and agency should part company or, if statutory orders do not permit that, reduce the extent of their contact to the minimum level consistent with a proper respect for the statutory order.

An Illustration: The Johnson Family

Having described each stage of the model, we wish to illustrate how it might apply in practice by tracing the progress of our agreement with the Johnson family through the various steps.

Mrs Johnson had been married to a man who was violent and aggressive towards her. She was young and had been educated in special (ESN(M)) school. After giving birth to her first child she found her husband being increasingly violent towards her. Andrew had been born with a slight heart defect and it was thought that he might suffer from a congenital syndrome which would result in delayed growth. A positive diagnosis was not possible.

At first, Andrew seemed to thrive but from the age of six months he stopped gaining weight and began to show other signs of developmental delay. At the same time the conflict in the parents' marriage was leading to a deterioration in the care he was receiving. The family's health visitor referred them to the Social Services Department. By this time the marriage was in crisis and Andrew was apparently suffering acute neglect. Mrs Johnson went with Andrew to a women's refuge but, soon after they were admitted, Andrew received a quite serious burn to his arm, apparently as a result of his mother's failure to protect him. A Place of Safety Order was obtained, followed by care proceedings when a Care Order was made.

Subsequently, Mrs Johnson formed a new relationship and she soon found herself pregnant. At the first statutory review on Andrew it was felt strongly that Mrs Johnson would not be able to cope with Andrew as well as the new baby. It was recommended that access should be terminated and that long-term foster-parents should be sought. Subsequently, the Social Services Department were advised by their solicitors that there were not sufficient grounds for the termination of access: if she contested the decision in court, Mrs Johnson would almost certainly obtain an order restoring access to her. At around this time, Mrs Johnson suffered a miscarriage and her solicitors threatened to apply for the revocation of the Care Order unless the Department reversed the plans it had made in the first review. Meanwhile Andrew, who had initially seemed to thrive in the care of the foster-parents, was going through another phase when he stopped gaining any weight and his general development seemed to come to a stop. No physiological explanation could be identified although doubts remained as to whether he was a physically well child.

At this point, Andrew's social worker approached the Family Service Unit and asked if we would be able to give Mrs Johnson and her new partner intensive support if the Department decided to send Andrew 'home on trial'. After we had indicated willingness to take on the work, we arranged with the social worker to be introduced to Mrs Johnson and her partner. In this Initial Contact stage we listened carefully to Mrs Johnson's account of her predicament. It was clear that she was very determined to secure the return of her son. Brian, her partner, said he would agree to anything to ensure that Andrew was allowed to come home.

As Andrew's mother was so keen to secure his return home and because the Department had already decided, albeit reluctantly and under pressure, that an attempt should be made to return Andrew to his mother, it seemed clear that the need was one our agency should try to meet. Therefore, we moved quickly on to stage 2 in our model. We needed to assess how much support Mrs Johnson would need with Andrew. We asked her, with Brian's help, to list the areas which she thought she would have difficulty with if Andrew came home. We also arranged to observe Andrew at the foster-parents' and subsequently to spend two hours at Mrs Johnson's house on a day when she had access to Andrew at home. These observations satisfied us that there was a degree of attachment between Andrew and his mother in spite of the nine months he had been in care. The list of the potential areas of difficulty which Mrs Johnson and Brian identified indicated that there was considerable awareness on their part that the process of rehabilitation would not be straightforward. The existence of a bond between mother and child, and the mother's recognition that she would need help encouraged us to think that the problem might be capable of resolution.

While engaged on stage 2 we were, at the same time, involved in identifying potential action-systems. Some of these were part of our own agency: a group for parents and small children who had encountered serious difficulties, and a project employing family aides to give intensive help when children were at risk of going into care. It was relatively easy to mobilise these. The Social Services Department retained the power to define access arrangements and to determine whether and, if so, when Andrew was allowed to return home. We, therefore, attended a meeting with the responsible Area Manager, the social worker who had referred Mrs Johnson to us, and Mrs Johnson and her solicitor. We outlined the package we thought we might be able to offer and established that, if the increased access we had in mind went well, the Social Services Department would allow Andrew to return 'home on trial' when we recommended it. Our aim was to increase access over a six week period, including overnight stays, until Mrs Johnson had the care of Andrew for a substantial portion of each week. This plan was discussed also with the foster-parents whose cooperation and consent was essential. They were doubtful at first but they were worried also about their own failure to make progress with Andrew's development and were prepared to explore any avenues which might improve things for him. They had come to recognise that his poor weight and developmental delay may have had an emotional rather than an exclusively physiological explanation.

Our final step in this stage was to establish that paediatric oversight would be offered. Having satisfied ourselves that the necessary resources would be available, and having obtained the basis of an agreement around a secondary contract with the Social Services Department, we were able to move on to stage 4 in which we identified an acceptable contract. It was clear that Mrs Johnson and Brian would accept almost any conditions in order to get Andrew back, and they seemed to understand the conditional nature of 'home on trial' arrangements. As our aim was the same as theirs and because the achievement of that aim would result in the successful completion of the work, the agreement we were seeking was a mutual mainstream agreement, primary rather than secondary. Establishing their willingness to participate seemed the easiest part of the negotiations. Therefore, we moved rapidly onto stage five in which a specific written contract was drawn up.

This contract set down the aim of our work together, namely to enable Mrs Johnson and Brian to care full-time for Andrew in a way that met his needs and enabled him to make appropriate developmental progress. We set out a schedule of gradually increased access which would be monitored by a Unit social worker who would seek also the foster-parents' reports on Andrew's reactions as access increased. Mrs Johnson and Brian were asked to agree to attend the group with Andrew each week as this coincided with one of their access visits. A target for Andrew's return home was fixed and we offered to arrange for the family aide to begin working with them, as soon as that date was reached, on the areas Mrs Johnson had herself identified as being problematic. These included toilet training, establishing a regular bed-time routine, and working out what sort of food to give him. When he had been taken away none of these had been issues which needed attention and Mrs Johnson realised that it would be difficult for her to tackle these areas when Andrew was not used to her being in a position of authority.

Once a draft contract had been prepared we were able to move on to the next stage of reaching agreement with the family. A meeting was held, attended by Mrs Johnson, Brian, the Unit social worker and family aide, and the local authority social worker. The local authority social worker expressed anxieties about the pace at which it was planned to return Andrew to his mother but was eventually prepared to go along with the agreement to which Mrs Johnson and Brian readily assented.

We were conscious that Mrs Johnson and Brian had very limited bargaining power at this stage: they knew that if they did not accept the terms which we offered, the only alternative would be to have recourse to the juvenile court, a slow and relatively inflexible procedure. Our own position was influenced by our awareness of the anxieties which had been expressed by the Social Services Department and the foster-parents. We had our own doubts since we still had very little first-hand experience of Mrs Johnson's parenting skills. When we moved on to stage 7, in which the work outlined in the agreement was undertaken, these difficulties surfaced quite quickly. Andrew settled surprisingly quickly at home and started putting on weight immediately. There were initial problems over a bed-time routine: Mrs Johnson was so pleased to have Andrew home that she found it very difficult to be firm with him. However, with help from the family aide, a reasonable routine was established eventually. Mrs Johnson and Andrew began attending the parent and toddler group although Brian only came once. However, within a few weeks, Mrs Johnson's attendance began to fall off. At first she could not bring herself to say directly that she did not wish to come but gave a variety of excuses.

The work which they had agreed to do at home with the family aide lasted a little longer: until, in fact, the difficulties of resuming those aspects of Andrew's care about which Mrs Johnson had been most anxious had been overcome. However, as soon as Mrs Johnson and Brian felt that they were managing to care for Andrew at a standard that was acceptable to them, they began to avoid the family aide. When she and the social worker arranged to meet with them, Brian was out. When a meeting was held several irrelevant issues were brought up in the meeting to avoid any serious discussion of our concern.

In the middle of all this, however, Andrew continued to thrive. Mrs Johnson allowed him to be seen by the paediatrician and, although his progress was not brilliant, it was an improvement on the latter period of his time in care. As the family seemed reluctant to implement their side of the agreement but because the aim of the agreement was being achieved, we decided to call a review. We were aware that, by this stage, there had been a substantial shift in the balance of power. Whereas, before Andrew had come home, the family had had very little room to negotiate, now that he was at home and doing relatively well, they were in a much stronger position to decide for themselves what help to accept and what to refuse. In the preparation for the review Brian was able to say how much he resented the extent that he and Mrs Johnson had to share their life and their home with social workers.

In stage 8, then, the progress which had been made towards the aim of re-establishing Andrew at home was summarised and the difficulties experienced by the unit workers in providing the level of support which had been agreed previously were spelled out. It was acknowledged that the family were doing better than we had anticipated, even though they were reluctant to make use of the services we could offer. A reduced level of support was offered, with the proviso that if this was unacceptable, we would have to withdraw from the work and ask the Social Services Department to take direct responsibility for supervising the care of Andrew. We were aware that they would only be prepared to take on a supervisory and monitoring role. Mrs Johnson and Brian negotiated with us on the package we were offering, much more selectively than at the initial stage of the work when Brian had said openly that he would accept any conditions in order to allow Andrew to return home. A new contract was agreed, rather different from the original agreement in that it was more reciprocal than mutual for Brian and Mrs Johnson's aim was now not merely to be able to resume the care of Andrew but to do this without interference from social workers.

These developments were only possible because Mrs Johnson and Brian had shown that they were able to give Andrew reasonable care. Had the Social Services Department removed Andrew because of the adults' reluctance to keep all parts of the agreement, Mrs Johnson would have had a reasonably strong case to apply for the revocation of the care order, whereas before he returned 'home on trial' it is likely that any application would have failed. Equally, we felt justified in trying to maintain as much input as possible since Andrew's development had been a pattern of progress followed by regression.

Conclusion

In practice it may not be possible always to work chronologically through the eight stages. It is acceptable, and often inevitable, to be engaged in several stages at once, especially in the exploratory phase of the work. However, this model does provide a framework of work to be done and, therefore, can bring some order to anxiety-provoking and complex situations. Indeed, where clients make heavy demands and present multiple problems, it is difficult to remain consistent and coherent without a framework and a focus and structure for the work. Through its emphasis on identifying the current situation, the desired situation, the focus of the work and the indicators to be used to assess progress towards the goals of the intervention, contracts can tackle what appear to be intractable problems and disentangle complex situations. Finally, the model is sufficiently flexible to be both able to home in on what is specific and to incorporate what will become clearer as the process develops.

Note

1. Linear causality is one model for explaining events and phenomena. It asserts 'if A, then B'. For example, if this stone hits a windscreen at a velocity of more than 30 miles per hour, the windscreen will shatter. In studying human relationships and other complex interactions, this model is often inadequate. The model of circular causality asserts 'if A, then B. If B, then A'. For example, if a boy's delinquent behaviour causes a certain reaction in law enforcement agencies, that reaction may result in the boy perceiving himself as a criminal who is expected to behave in a delinquent way. This leads to more delinquent acts and more powerful reactions from the police and courts. Obviously, this cycle may perpetuate itself until some other intervention breaks the pattern. Equifinality rejects the idea that social phenomena can be understood by employing a simple linear model and allows instead for the possibility that apparently identical phenomena may result from quite different combinations of causal factors; and that the same causal factors, operating on very similar systems, may yet result in quite different outcomes. For example, two people of very similar background may react quite differently to a bereavement. Equally, two people who present identical depressive symptoms cannot be assumed to have been affected by the same, or even a similar, causal pattern. The implication which follows from this is that there can be no one 'correct' intervention in these circumstances which will relieve the suffering.

7 Contracts: A Practice Concept for Social Workers?

Introduction

In our experience various issues lead practitioners to doubt the feasibility and applicability of using contracts. These issues centre on images and fantasies of contracts, on perceptions of the nature of client–worker relationships, and of the practice demands on social workers. This chapter will consider these issues, not to pretend that easy or universal answers exist, but to convey our belief that difficulties or doubts about using contracts in social work practice are not insurmountable. Some points, made in earlier chapters, are reiterated here when they offer a means of surmounting the obstacle.

Time-consuming?

One image is that using contracts is time-consuming, involving either the need for more regular contact than practitioners have space to provide or additional work in exploring the basis for and drawing up an agreement. We believe that this is a misconception. The practice skills required have much in common with those already familiar to social workers: assessment, negotiation of problem-definition, allocation of tasks, review and evaluation. Indeed, agreements akin to contracts develop all the time, but usually in an implicit and unrecognised way. Contract-based practice aims to use these skills more systematically by placing them into a framework for identifying what the work is, when the work is in progress, evaded or concluded, and whether the outcome of the change process has achieved the stated goals.

This may represent a change in the use of client-worker time and in the content of client–worker interaction, but it does not follow necessarily from this that extra time demands will be placed on practitioners. Indeed, this approach can answer some of the criticisms of contemporary social work and make a positive contribution to an environment of overstretched workloads, increasing demands and decreasing resources.

Because of the pressure of work, social workers often find themselves having to respond in an unplanned way, dictated by crises and emergencies. Their work is then pervaded with a sense of the inevitability and intractability of client problems and with minimal expectations for change. Many attempts at change become bogged down and the original problems or goals are obscured. This chronic state of affairs is determined partly by the expectations placed on social workers by society and partly by a lack of clarity about what the problem is, for whom it is a problem, what change is needed or wanted and how participants would know that the work has been accomplished. It is shaped also by perceptions of pathology, seen still as residing mainly in the individual, and of clienthood as a state rather than a transition. A clash in perspective is not uncommon between practitioners and consumers both in respect of the aims of intervention and the type of authority underpinning it. For example, a client may define the social worker's authority as deriving from their professional position and their agency obligations, whereas the practitioner may rely on the authority they feel they have acquired through their experience of handling similar situations in the past. The absence of clear, agreed aims and this clash of perspective are time consuming since they reduce social work's impact and effectiveness.

There is also dissatisfaction with the level of dependence which some social work methods create (Smith and Corden, 1981), leading to self-perpetuating caseloads and reduced opportunities for undertaking new work. Not only can this perpetual, almost compulsive care-giving reduce client autonomy and engender dependency and hostility, but also it can disable social workers and render agencies inefficient and unproductive.

Good practice deserves time and a climate where the emphasis is on quality not quantity. We believe that contracts assist workers to achieve higher standards of practice and to question old, reflex reactions and habitual practices (Sheldon, 1980). They offer a framework for focusing practice by mapping out the targets for intervention, the tasks of the participants and the role of reviews. This approach can prove an effective method for time-limited and time-limiting work but, even where it does not save time, many clients seem to find agreements helpful and appreciate the collaborative relationship involving clearly stated goals and agreed sharing of tasks (Preston-Shoot, 1985). We believe that the effectiveness of this approach comes additionally from the fact that the parties know the direction of their change efforts and combine their efforts to reach their goals more quickly by avoiding the frustration, anger and confusion generated by double agendas (Munday, 1978; Mullender, 1979). It increases task performance too, since making commitments explicit produces some pressure to honour the agreement and produce results from the relationship (Rimmer, 1978).

Over-formal and Threatening?

Some social workers believe that clients are likely to perceive contracts as official, over-formal and potentially threatening. Initially, clients may be suspicious of contracts, perhaps perceiving them in legalistic terms; or they may be wary of social workers' motives. Contracts might seem like another social work game, without real significance. However, if some clients find the change difficult, others may feel less threatened, finding it easier to accept an agreement which limits their commitment and exposure to professionals.

Whatever the client's reaction, some form of role induction may be helpful: introducing the idea to ensure that the participants understand the relevance of and rationale behind the approach. Several explanations may be needed of the concept and its purpose, that is the ethos and value principles informing its use and the structure: initial definitions of objectives, roles for worker/client, reviews and measures of progress. This role induction should include addressing feelings clients may hold about the change, especially where the approach is being introduced to consumers who have been used to a different approach previously since they, rather than new consumers, are more likely to find the change and its implications difficult to negotiate (Smith and Corden, 1981). This role induction does help clients to engage providing that the language used and explanations given are simple and honest.

Arguably, social workers may find the concept at least as threatening as clients. Since a contractual approach requires that consumers be involved in defining the problems and targets for change, taking on their views may lead social workers to face questions which they have previously avoided. Moreover, this method does involve a degree of openness concerning aims which, in some contexts such as child abuse, social workers may find difficult. Equally, where the approach is innovative rather than established practice, they may suppose that colleagues will scorn the idea or be quick to criticise apparent failure. Whilst personal commitment to the concept and the values underpinning it is essential, so too is the support and understanding of colleagues. Alternatively, workers may feel an increased sense of 'stuckness' if the work is not progressing and a contract exists. However, this need not always be a cause for pessimism. The concept of review allows participants to explore the meaning of the 'stuckness', the information it gives and possible alterations to the contract.

Dependency

Some practitioners have questioned us on whether contracts encourage dependency or involve replacing one form of drift with another. We believe that the opposite is true providing that contracts do not become ritualised pseudo-agreements entered into by consumers to avoid embarrassment or to receive particular services (Macarov, 1974). Our view is based on the belief that a contract-based approach provides an escape from a situation where social workers, dependent on resources provided by society, feel themselves to be progressively sucked dry by clients who depend on them for sustenance; and where clients experience this relationship in a similar unsatisfactory way, unhappy at being on the receiving end of a unilateral gift relationship, a one-way relationship which encourages dependency and keeps clients under professional power and control (Corden, 1980). The escape is that both participants may withdraw from a non-useful association without feeling rejected or rejecting.

Dependency has many causes, including:
1. Defensive social work, creating conservative practice, arising from practitioners and managers seeing the media, inquiries and the possibility of tragedy as shadows behind each client.
2. The historical influence of psychoanalysis, where symptoms are defined as illness/pathology rather than the emphasis being on an individual's capacity for self-direction.
2. The relative neglect of social change goals, where social workers have yet to find effective ways of addressing the social, economic and political faces of the difficulties which clients face privately.
2. Stereotypes of problem families which limit expectations of change.
5. A total solution approach to social work, involving an expectation of complete cure, rather than the provision of a new impetus alone. To use a metaphor, the difference is between providing a motorist who has broken down with every conceivable assistance to complete a journey, and simply repairing the faulty part of the car.

A contract approach seeks to prevent the creation or maintenance of dependency by:
1. Involving clients in the task of defining and implementing the change effort, thereby offering them greater opportunities for self-direction. The approach sees clients as active, involved, determining persons, capable of defining their needs and rights and of choosing between alternatives.
2. Emphasising movement and freeing the situation. The accent is on change and growth.
3. Defining the relationship as time-limited.
4. Seeking to remove double-agendas by sharing the definition and elaboration of the target problems and goals.
5. Ensuring that the social worker is less central to the change process by structuring and organising the work so that roles and expectations are defined and the client's self-esteem, motivation and investment are enhanced by having a real say in proceedings.

The evidence is that many clients welcome this more equal partnership and that consumers are able to assume control of more aspects of their lives and reduce their dependency on social workers (Smith and Corden, 1981; Mullender and Ward, 1985; Preston-Shoot, 1985). This is not to imply that it is never appropriate to meet dependency needs but that this should follow from a dialogue which determines what the situation is, the available options, and a choice acceptable to each party. It should be a joint decision, based on a shared recognition that greater independence is not achievable, rather than a collusive compliance with minimal consensus between the parties (Hutten, 1974).

Inflexibility

Some social workers have questioned whether contracts can be sufficiently flexible and responsive to changing needs and situations. We believe that this doubt comes from perceiving contracts as legalistic, fixed entities rather than as the framework for a process of negotiation, review and renegotiation. Just as families often experience difficulties when there are no rules to change rules, so social workers and their clients need a framework within which changes can be agreed in their rules which govern their relationship. Contracts, like any form of social work intervention, should be a developing phenomenon, reviewed throughout and, if necessary, renegotiated.

Contracts can be adapted in response to unforeseen changes in circumstances or crises which necessitate a change in the focus of the intervention providing these changes are seen as information requiring a review to examine the possibility of varying the contract. Where crises are frequent, they can provide information to help assess whether the objectives in the agreement are realistic and the intervention appropriate. There are obvious dangers in constant renegotiation but a sequence of short-term agreements is more useful than soldiering on with one which has outlived its usefulness.

There are dangers too when the contract becomes the goal rather than the means of attaining the goals or when working on the problems is delayed or avoided, that is when focus on the work is lost through concentrating on the task of seeking an agreement. Certainly, social workers using contracts need to guard against becoming too task-oriented, too preoccupied with making the contract. This will be easier if they follow the step-by-step model we have outlined and if they are clear about the circumstances in each situation which would necessitate variation, review or termination.

One-sided?

This criticism originates from the word 'contract' which implies an agreed basis for working in which both parties have participated freely. The critics point out that such a relationship, which gives a sense of meaningful participation derived from a shared experience, is difficult to achieve within client–worker relationships. The client–worker relationship is often one of unequal power. The social worker wields considerable positional, organisational and sapiential authority and can underestimate and under-use the authority of the client. The critics also point out that contracts in social work cannot be legally binding and that clients' rights of appeal are limited at best. Moreover, it is not unusual for there to be disagreement between members of the client-system about what the problems are and about who needs to change what, or for the client-system to disagree with the social worker's view. Therefore, can contracts really be two-sided agreements or are they just a form of open casework at best or a means of control and a sham and pretence at worst?

How might social workers demonstrate a wish to actually share the power and responsibility which traditionally they retain? We suggest the following as useful rules of thumb: thumb:

1. Openly acknowledge the power relationship and discuss the type of authority you wish to exercise and the consumer perceives you using.
2. State what you can offer and what might be expected of the client. For clients to be in a strong position when negotiating the contract, they must know what they can expect.
3. State whom the client might turn to if the contract is broken by the social worker. This requires not only a formal review procedure but a complaints procedure to which the client has full, direct access.
4. Build in and make clear the responsibility of the social worker for carrying out their part of the agreement. What has the social worker contracted to do?
5. Build in and make clear the responsibility of the client for carrying out their part of the agreement. What has the client agreed to do?
6. Only promise what you feel you can deliver. Only enter agreements which you are able to carry out. For example, where a client has expressed a wish to remain in the community, under what circumstances would the social worker feel unable to support the client in that decision?
7. Address any pressures on the client to comply. Ensure that the client is not agreeing to avoid the loss of services or because of the worker's status or expertise.
8. Specify as explicitly as possible the nature of the transaction, especially the goals and roles of the parties and the limits to the contract. For example, in statutory work, the worker's authority function should be separated from an invitation to work together on specific problems.
9. Ensure that aims are realistic and feasible since this gives clients a better basis for accepting an offer and for making alternative or supplementary suggestions.
10. Do not impose your agenda or definition of the problem on the

client. All the parties should be invited to share their assessment of what contributes to the problem.

Where members of the client–system disagree amongst themselves or with the worker, one approach is to agree on a specific goal, about which there is agreement, in the hope that this will enable the conditions to be set for agreement on other areas to be found later. A second approach is to focus entirely on the client's requests for help. A third is to establish each participant's views regarding each aspect of the problem, to find agreement on some targets and to explore the possibility of a reciprocal agreement to cover the areas where there is disagreement. This may require social workers to summarise the content of interviews, to highlight similarities and differences between the views of the participants and to use their authority and influence to draw clients' attention to aspects of the problem of which they may be unaware. The purpose is not to insist on this definition of the problem if clients do not respond positively to workers' suggestions but to express differing views and aim for an agreement to which all parties can commit themselves (Corden, 1980; Smith and Corden, 1981).

This method of working can be applied to statutory work, that aspect of social work where the power and authority imbalance is most marked. Clearly the client is to some extent a captive, where the risk of non-compliance or mock-compliance is high, and where the social worker cannot assume, at the beginning of the work, that the conditions exist for a contract as the client is not yet a client in the sense of asking for help. Nor, if the social worker breaches their part of the contract, can the client sever the relationship as they can in other types of client–worker relationship, but the client can exercise self-direction and autonomy concerning whether or not they work out a plan with the social worker for working together on specific problems. Nor, when all the objectives within a contract formed as a result of a supervision order or non-accidental injury of a child have been achieved, can the worker guarantee that the aim of de-registration or revoking the order will be realised, because this depends ultimately on the assent of other parties. Moreover, a worker's responsibilities to other systems and to their agency may limit what they can agree with clients. What is required, therefore, is honesty and planning, openness with each other and shared goal setting. Workers must state clearly what they can offer, making their agency obligations explicit since they may not be able to determine the outcome of statutory intervention, even where the contract is completed successfully. However, they should try to specify what will happen after the successful completion of a contract and the circumstances in which they would invoke the powers available to them.

Breakdown
Many social workers are particularly concerned about the sanctions

which would be available when a contract breaks down. They feel that they have little to bargain with and that to be meaningful a breach must incur some form of loss. However, they appear to have difficulty in exercising their option of rescission, even where there is no statutory requirement for continued intervention, which leaves them feeling that a contract which has broken down has created a more intractable situation than if a contract had not existed. We feel that the approach towards sanctions and breakdowns should take account of five points:

1. It may be difficult at the outset to know what to realistically expect and expectations set may have to be modified in the light of experience.
2. Think about the consequences of non-fulfilment when the agreement is made since, if not considered then, the problem of non-compliance will be compounded by a heightened sense of powerlessness on the social worker's part.
3. Approach breakdown not as a case for termination but as positive material for future work. The first question, therefore, is what is the meaning of the breakdown. For example, are the aims relevant to the client? Is the client too fearful to participate in the way agreed? Workers can extract information from breakdown or non-performance within an agreement. It may not be a sign of resistance but rather a message about how clients do things which, if used as such, can enable workers and clients to develop a cooperative relationship.
4. Distinguish between breakdown which results from disagreement about aims and that which results from failure of the means employed. Where it becomes apparent that disagreements exist between clients or between workers and clients, this may be because the client is not yet a real client, either because there has been no request for help, or because the client is unsure what the intervention may involve. It may reflect disagreement about what needs to change. For example, practitioners may locate the area for change within the client-system, whereas the clients may target systems beyond themselves. There may be agreement about what needs to change but disagreement on how that change should be achieved. Finally, the disagreement may be founded on one party's inability to enter into the agreement, for example because of agency limitations in terms of resources, or obligations to other systems.
5. Consider 'what if...' questions, what might happen in the event of the agreement not being honoured in part or in full. Answers to these questions will depend on the context of the interaction between the participants. Their importance lies in enabling the work to be undertaken effectively on the basis of clearly agreed rules. The following 'what if...' questions point to what should not be overlooked:

(a) What if a family or group member requests an interview between arranged sessions?

(b) What if someone is not there whom you have asked to be present?

(c) What if someone present leaves the room?

(d) What if someone telephones to say that a child in the family has a bruise?

(e) What if a family member telephones to say that the family does not want to come any more?

(f) What if the agreed contract is for sessions lasting one hour and the client arrives very late?

(g) What if you visit as arranged and no-one is in or someone is present who was not invited?

(h) What if group members decline to join in agreed activities?

(i) What if clients want to add something to an already agreed programme?

(j) What if another agency which has agreed to a secondary contract with you and your clients acts precipitately outside that agreement?

(k) What if an emergency arises elsewhere when you have an arranged session?

Conclusion

Contracts are not a panacea for all the difficulties faced by social workers. Nor would we wish to underestimate the importance of such qualities as warmth and acceptance in successful interventions. However, we believe they can improve efficiency and bring focus and meaning to basic social work values and principles. They are not necessarily difficult to maintain and they can enhance motivation, clarify what problems are being tackled and bring order and structure to the intervention. As such, they are a counter to dependency and a tool with which to evaluate the effectiveness of social work. Most importantly, they involve the client in the process of determining the change effort and the social worker in making explicit their intentions and methods of working. This may be especially useful when there is some distance between the client's aims and the worker's, when there are different views within the client system and when mistrust and hostility surround the social worker's intervention.

Our purpose has been to give practitioners a sense that using contracts in their practice is feasible and important. Even where they do not use explicit contracts with their clients, we believe that having the conceptual framework to hand will help to guide social workers through their interactions with consumers and other systems.

Bibliography

Barclay, P. (ed.) (1982) *Social Workers, Their Role and Tasks*, London, Bedford Square Press.

BASW (1980) *Clients are Fellow Citizens*, Birmingham, British Association of Social Workers.

BASW (1983) *Effective and Ethical Recording*, Birmingham, British Association of Social Workers.

Barton, R. (1966) *Institutional Neurosis*, Bristol, John Wright and Sons.

Beckford Report (1985) *A Child in Trust. The Report of the Inquiry into the Death of Jasmine Beckford*, London Borough of Brent.

Berridge, D. (1985) *Residential Children's Homes*, Oxford, Basil Blackwell.

Bland, R. and Bland, R.E. (1985) ' "Contract" and admission to old people's homes', *British Journal of Social Work*, 15(2), 133–42.

Bottoms, A. and McWilliams, W. (1979) 'A non-treatment paradigm for probation practice', *British Journal of Social Work*, 9(2), 159–202.

Bowlby, J. (1951) *Maternal Care and Mental Health*, London, World Health Organisation.

Brake, M. and Bailey, R. (eds) (1980) *Radical Social Work and Practice*, London, Edward Arnold.

Burck, C. (1978) 'A study of families' expectations and experiences of a child guidance clinic', *British Journal of Social Work*, 8(2), 145–58.

Butler, J., Bow, I. and Gibbons, J. (1978) 'Task-centred casework with marital problems', *British Journal of Social Work*, 8(4), 393–410.

Campbell, T.D. (1978) 'Discretionary rights' in Timms, N. and Watson, D. (eds) *Philosophy in Social Work*, London, Routledge & Kegan Paul.

Carew, R. (1979) 'The place of knowledge in social work', *British Journal of Social Work*, 9(3), 349–64.

Centre for Policy on Ageing (1984) *Home Life*, London, Working Party on a Code of Practice for Residential Care.

Corden, J. (1976) 'The hostel as a learning environment', in Peryer, D., Brandon, D. and Corden, J. *Residential Care*, London, National Association for the Care and Resettlement of Offenders.

Corden, J. (1980) 'Contracts in social work practice', *British Journal of Social Work*, 10(2), 143–62.

Corrigan, P. and Leonard, P. (1978) *Social Work Practice under Capitalism: A Marxist Approach*, London, Macmillan.

Coulshed, V. (1980) 'A unitary approach to the care of the hospitalised elderly mentally ill', *British Journal of Social Work*, 10(1), 19–32.

Curnock, K. and Hardiker, P. (1979) *Towards Practice Theory: Skills and Methods in Social Assessments*, London, Routledge & Kegan Paul.

Currie, R. and Parrott, B. (1981) *A Unitary Approach to Social Work— Application in Practice*, Birmingham, British Association of Social Workers.

Davies, F.R. (1970) *Contract*, London, Sweet and Maxwell.

Davies, M. (1981) *The Essential Social Worker*, London, Heinemann.

Day, P.R. (1981) *Social Work and Social Control*, London, Routledge & Kegan Paul.

DHSS (1983) *Personal Social Services Records—Disclosure of Information to Clients*, LAC (83)14.

Epstein, I. (1975) 'The politics of behaviour therapy: The new cool-out casework' in Jones H. (ed.) *Towards A New Social Work*, London, Routledge & Kegan Paul.

FSU (1982) *Family Involvement in the Social Work Process*, London, Family Service Units.

FSU (1984) *Family Involvement: Access and Participation*, London, Family Service Units.

FSU (1985) *Access to Records*, London, Family Service Units.

Fischer, J.L. and Gochros, H.L. (1975) *Planned Behaviour Change: Behaviour Modification in Social Work*, London, Collier-Macmillan.

Fisher, M. (ed.) (1983) *Speaking of Clients*, Sheffield, Joint Unit for Social Services Research.

Gambrill, E. (1977) *Behaviour Modification: Handbook of Assessment, Intervention and Evaluation*, San Francisco, Jossey-Bass.

Garvin, C. (1969) 'The complementarity of role expectations in groups: the member–worker contract', in *Social Work Practice 1969*, 127–45. New York, Columbia University Press.

Gibbons, J., Bow, I., Butler, J. and Powell, J. (1979) 'Clients' reactions to task-centred casework: a follow-up study', *British Journal of Social Work*, 9(2), 203–16.

Gibbons, J., Bow, I. and Butler, J. (1985) 'Task-centred social work after parasuicide', in Goldberg, E.M., Gibbons, J. and Sinclair, I. (eds) *Problems, Tasks and Outcomes: The Evaluation of Task-centred Casework in Three Settings*, London, Allen and Unwin.

Goffman, E. (1961) *Asylums*, Harmondsworth, Penguin Books.

Goldberg, E.M. and Robinson, J. (1977) 'An area office of an English Social Services Department', in Reid, W.J. and Epstein, L. (eds) *Task-centred Practice*, New York, Columbia University Press.

Goldfarb, W. (1945) 'Effects of psychological deprivation in infancy and subsequent stimulation', *American Journal of Orthopsychiatry*, 102, 18–33.

Goldstein, H. (1973) *Social Work Practice: A Unitary Approach*, Columbia, University of South Carolina Press.

Griffiths, W.A. (1970) *After-Care Hostels: A Critique of the Family*

Model, London, National Association for the Care and Resettlement of Offenders.

Hall, E.S. (1980) 'Collecting and using data for assessment', in Walton, R. and Elliott, D. (eds) *Residential Care: A Reader in Current Theory and Practice*, Oxford, Pergamon Press.

Herbert, M. (1981) *Behavioural Treatment of Problem Children: A Practice Manual*, London, Academic Press.

Hine, J., McWilliams, W. and Pease, K. (1978) 'Recommendations, social information and sentencing', *Howard Journal of Penology and Crime Prevention*, xvii, 91–100.

Holborn, J. (1975) 'Casework with short-term prisoners', in *Some Male Offenders' Problems*, London, Home Office Research Unit. No. 28, London, HMSO.

Holder, D. and Wardle, M. (1981) *Teamwork and the Development of a Unitary Approach*, London, Routledge & Kegan Paul.

Howe, D. (1979) 'Agency function and social work principles', *British Journal of Social Work*, 9(1), 29–48.

Hutten, J. (1974) 'Short-term contracts', *Social Work Today*, 4(22), 709–11.

Jones, H. (ed.) (1975) *Towards A New Social Work*, London, Routledge & Kegan Paul.

Liebmann, M. (1980) 'Contracting into an ordered lifestyle', *Social Work Today*, 11(30), 16–17.

Lishman, J. (1978) 'A clash in perspective? A study of worker and client perceptions of social work', *British Journal of Social Work*, 8(3), 301–12.

Macarov, D. (1974) 'Client–worker agreement: Necessity, desideratum, or dogma?', *Social Work Today*, 4(24), 773–6.

Maluccio, A. and Marlow, W. (1974) 'The case for the contract', *Social Work (USA)*, 19(1), 28–36.

Mayer, J. and Timms, N. (1970) *The Client Speaks*, London, Routledge & Kegan Paul.

McAuley, R. and McAuley, P. (1980) 'The effectiveness of behaviour modification with families', *British Journal of Social Work*, 10(1), 43–54.

McKay, A., Goldberg, E.M. and Fruin, D.J. (1973) 'Consumers and a Social Services Department', *Social Work Today*, 4(16), 486–9.

Middleman, R. and Goldberg, G. (1974) *Social Service Delivery: A Structural Approach To Social Work Practice*, New York, Columbia University Press.

Miller, E.J. and Gwynne, G.V. (1975) *A Life Apart*, London, Tavistock.

Mullender, A. (1979) 'Drawing up a more democratic contract', *Social Work Today*, 11(11), 17–18.

Mullender, A. and Ward, D. (1985) 'Towards an alternative model of social groupwork', *British Journal of Social Work*, 15(2), 155–72.

Munday, B. (1978) 'The potentials and pitfalls of short-term contract work', *Social Work Today*, 9(43), 23.

NCVO. (1985) *Clients' Rights*, Report of a Working Party, London, National Council of Voluntary Organisations/Bedford Square Press.

Norman, A. (1980) *Rights and Risks*, London, National Corporation for the Care of Old People.

O'Brien, D. (1979) 'From residential unit to day assessment centre', *Social Work Today*, 10(27), 26–9.

Page, R. and Clark, G. (1977) *Who Cares? Young People in Care Speak Out*, London, National Children's Bureau.

Parker, H., Casburn, M. and Turnbull, D. (1981) *Receiving Juvenile Justice*, Oxford, Basil Blackwell.

PSSC (1975) *Living and Working in Residential Homes*, London, Personal Social Services Council.

Phillimore, P. (1981) *Families Speaking*, London, Family Service Units.

Phillimore, P. (1982) 'Some comments on the interpretation of clienthood', *FSU Quarterly*, 26, 37–43.

Pincus, A. and Minahan, A. (1973) *Social Work Practice: Model and Method*, Itasca, New York, Peacock Press.

Plant, R. (1970) *Social and Moral Theory in Casework*, London, Routledge & Kegan Paul.

Preston-Shoot, M., Corden, J. and Ennis, J. (1984) 'The making and breaking of contracts', *FSU Quarterly*, 33, 17–24.

Preston-Shoot, M. (1985) 'An evaluation of a policy of family involvement in one FSU from the families' perspective', *FSU Quarterly*, 36, 52–64.

Preston-Shoot, M. (1987) *Effective Groupwork*, London, Macmillan.

Rees, S. (1978) *Social Work Face To Face*, London, Edward Arnold.

Rees, S. and Wallace A. (1982) *Verdicts on Social Work*, London, Edward Arnold.

Reid, W.J. (1978) *The Task-centred System*, New York, Columbia University Press.

Reid, W.J. and Epstein, L. (1972) *Task-centred Casework*, New York, Columbia University Press.

Reid, W.J. and Shyne, A. (1969) *Brief and Extended Casework*, New York, Columbia University Press.

Reinach, E. and Roberts, G. (1979) *Consequences*, Portsmouth Social Services Research and Intelligence Unit.

Rimmer, J. (1978) ' "Contract" and other interlopers in social work', in Olsen, R. (ed.) *The Unitary Model*, Birmingham, British Association of Social Workers.

Robinson, T. (1978) *In Worlds Apart: Professionals and Clients in the Welfare State*, London, Bedford Square Press.

Sainsbury, E. (1975) *Social Work With Families*, London, Routledge & Kegan Paul.

Sainsbury, E., Nixon, S. and Phillips, D. (1982) *Social Work in Focus*,

London, Routledge & Kegan Paul.

Shaw, I. (1976) 'Consumer opinion and social policy: A research review', *Journal of Social Policy*, 5(1), 19–32.

Shaw, I. (1984) 'Literature review. Consumer evaluations of the personal social services', *British Journal of Social Work*, 14(3), 277–84.

Shaw, M. and Lebens, K. (1977) 'Foster-parents talking', *Adoption and Fostering*, 88, 11–16.

Sheldon, B. (1978) 'Theory and practice in social work: a re-examination of a tenuous relationship', *British Journal of Social Work*, 8(1), 1–22.

Sheldon, B. (1980) *The Use of Contracts in Social Work*, Birmingham, British Association of Social Workers.

Sheldon, B. (1982) *Behaviour Modification: Theory, Practice and Philosophy*, London, Tavistock.

Simpkin, M. (1979) *Trapped Within Welfare. Surviving Social Work*, London, Macmillan.

Skynner, A.C.R. (1976) *One Flesh: Separate Persons*, London, Constable.

Smale, G. (1977) *Prophecy, Behaviour and Change*, London, Routledge & Kegan Paul.

Smalley, R. (1970) 'The functional approach to casework practice', in Roberts, R. and Nee, R. (eds) *Theories of Social Casework*, Chicago, University of Chicago Press.

Smith, G. and Corden, J. (1981) 'The introduction of contracts in a Family Service Unit', *British Journal of Social Work*, 11(3), 289–314.

Spitz, R. (1945) 'Hospitalism: an inquiry into the genesis of psychiatric conditions in early childhood' *Psychoanalytic Study of the Child*, 1.

Spitz, R. (1946) 'Anaclitic depression', *Psychoanalytic Study of the Child*. 2.

Statham, D. (1978) *Radicals in Social Work*, London, Routledge & Kegan Paul.

Taft, J. (1937) 'The relation of function to process in social case work', *Journal of Social Work Process*, 1, 3.

Thoburn, J. (1980) *Captive Clients: Social Work with Families of Children Home on Trial*, London, Routledge & Kegan Paul.

Thorpe, J. and Pease, K. (1976) 'The relationship between recommendations made to the court and sentences passed', *British Journal of Criminology*, 16(4), 393–4.

Truax, C. and Carkhuff, R. (1967) *Towards Effective Counselling and Psychotherapy*, Chicago, Aldine.

Walker, H. and Beaumont, W. (eds) (1981) *Probation Work: Critical Theory and Socialist Practice*, Oxford, Basil Blackwell.

Ward, E. (1980) 'The social work task in residential care', in Walton R. and Elliott, D. (eds) *Residential Care: A Reader in Current Theory and Practice*, Oxford, Pergamon Press.

Whittington, C. (1971) 'Self-determination re-examined', *British Journal of Social Work*, 1(3), 293–303.

Whittington, C. (1983) 'Social work in the welfare network: Negotiating daily practice', *British Journal of Social Work*, 13(3), 265–86.

Index